slices

a fine selection of sweet treats

MURDOCH BOOKS

Contents

Dear friends

Take a trip down memory lane with these old-fashioned favourites.

Fig and cinnamon slice

MAKES 15

125 g (4½ oz/½ cup) unsalted butter, softened
55 g (2 oz) soft brown sugar
1 teaspoon ground cinnamon
185 g (6½ oz/1½ cups) plain (all-purpose) flour, sifted
375 g (13 oz) dried figs
1 cinnamon stick
115 g (4 oz/½ cup) caster (superfine) sugar
375 ml (13 fl oz/1½ cups) boiling water

Preheat the oven to 180°C (350°F/Gas 4). Lightly grease an 18 x 28 cm (7 x 11¼ inch) baking tin and line the base with baking paper, extending the paper over the long sides for easy removal later.

Beat the butter, brown sugar and ground cinnamon in a medium bowl with electric beaters until light and fluffy. Fold in the flour with a large metal spoon. Press the mixture evenly into the prepared tin and bake for 25 minutes. Cool slightly.

Combine the figs, cinnamon stick, caster sugar and water in a saucepan and bring to the boil. Reduce the heat to low and simmer for 20 minutes, or until the figs have softened and the liquid has reduced by one-third. Remove the cinnamon stick and place the mixture in the bowl of a food processor. Process in short bursts until smooth. Pour onto the cooked base and bake for 10 minutes, or until set. Cool in the tin and when cold, lift out and cut into squares.

Raspberry and coconut slice

MAKES 12

280 g (10 oz/2¼ cups) plain (all-purpose) flour
3 tablespoons ground almonds
450 g (1 lb/2 cups) caster (superfine) sugar
250 g (9 oz/1 cup) unsalted butter, chilled and
   cut into cubes
½ teaspoon ground nutmeg
½ teaspoon baking powder
4 eggs
1 teaspoon natural vanilla extract
1 tablespoon lemon juice
300 g (10½ oz) fresh or thawed
   frozen raspberries
90 g (3¼ oz/1 cup) desiccated coconut
icing (confectioners') sugar, sifted, for dusting

Preheat the oven to 180°C (350°F/Gas 4). Lightly grease a 20 x 30 cm (8 x 12 inch) baking tin and line the base with baking paper, extending the paper over the long sides for easy removal later.

Sift 220 g (7¾ oz/1¾ cups) of the flour into a large bowl. Add the almonds and 115 g (4 oz/½ cup) of the caster sugar and stir to combine. Rub in the butter with your fingertips until the mixture resembles fine breadcrumbs. Press into the prepared tin and bake for 20–25 minutes, or until golden.

Reduce the oven temperature to 150°C (300°F/Gas 2).

Sift the nutmeg, baking powder and the remaining flour onto a piece of baking paper. Beat the eggs, vanilla and the remaining caster sugar in a large bowl with electric beaters for 4 minutes, or until light and creamy. Fold in the flour mixture with a large metal spoon. Stir in the lemon juice, raspberries and coconut, then pour over the base. Bake for 1 hour, or until golden. You may need to cover with foil if the top browns too quickly. Set aside to cool in the tin, then cut into pieces. Dust with the icing sugar and serve.

Macadamia fingers

180 g (6¼ oz) unsalted butter, softened
1 teaspoon natural vanilla extract
80 g (2¾ oz/⅓ cup) caster (superfine) sugar
250 g (9 oz/2 cups) plain (all-purpose)
flour, sifted

Topping
125 g (4½ oz/½ cup) unsalted butter
2 x 400 g (14 oz) tins condensed milk
2 tablespoons golden syrup (light treacle)
200 g (7 oz/1¼ cups) macadamia nuts,
coarsely chopped

Preheat the oven to 180°C (350°F/Gas 4). Lightly grease a 20 x 30 cm (8 x 12 inch) baking tin and line the base and sides with baking paper, extending the paper over the long sides for easy removal later.

Place the butter, vanilla and sugar in a large bowl and cream with electric beaters until pale and fluffy. Stir in the flour and mix until well combined. Press the mixture firmly and evenly into the prepared tin and bake for 25 minutes, or until the base is cooked and a little browned. Cool slightly.

To make the topping, place the butter, condensed milk and golden syrup in a saucepan and stir over low heat until the butter has melted. Increase the heat to medium and stir constantly for 15–20 minutes, or until the mixture is thick and caramel-like. Add the macadamias and pour onto the biscuit base. Bake for 10 minutes, or until golden. Cool in the tin. Remove from the tin, cut in half lengthways, then cut into fingers and serve.

Choc honeycomb slice

MAKES 18

100 g (3½ oz) unsalted butter, roughly chopped
300 g (10½ oz) milk chocolate, roughly chopped
115 g (4 oz/⅓ cup) golden syrup (light treacle)
200 g (7 oz) digestive biscuits (cookies), roughly
  broken up
100 g (3½ oz) honeycomb, roughly broken up

Lightly grease a 16 x 26 cm (6¼ x 10½ inch) baking tin and line the base and sides with baking paper, extending the paper over the long sides for easy removal later.

Place the butter, chocolate and golden syrup in a saucepan. Cook, stirring occasionally, over low heat for 5 minutes, or until the chocolate has melted. Stir through the biscuits and honeycomb. Pour into the prepared tin and use a spatula to smooth the top. Refrigerate until set. Cut into pieces and serve.

Sesame and ginger slice

MAKES 15

125 g (4½ oz/1 cup) plain (all-purpose) flour
½ teaspoon bicarbonate of soda (baking soda)
1 teaspoon ground ginger
¼ teaspoon mixed (pumpkin pie) spice
2 eggs
140 g (5 oz/¾ cup) soft brown sugar
125 g (4½ oz/½ cup) unsalted butter, melted and cooled
55 g (2 oz/¼ cup) chopped crystallised ginger
50 g (1¾ oz/⅓ cup) sesame seeds, toasted

Preheat the oven to 180°C (350°F/Gas 4). Lightly grease a 20 x 30 cm (8 x 12 inch) baking tin and line the base with baking paper, extending the paper over the long sides for easy removal later.

Sift the flour, bicarbonate of soda, ground ginger, mixed spice and ¼ teaspoon of salt onto a sheet of baking paper. Beat the eggs and brown sugar in a large bowl for 2 minutes, or until thick and creamy. Mix in the melted butter and gently fold in the flour mixture. Add the crystallised ginger and half the sesame seeds, and mix gently.

Pour the mixture into the prepared tin, smooth the top with a spatula and scatter the remaining sesame seeds over the top. Bake for 20 minutes, or until firm to touch and lightly golden. Cool in the tin for 10 minutes, then transfer to a wire rack to cool completely. Cut into pieces and serve.

Peach and sour cream slice

MAKES 15

150 g (5½ oz) unsalted butter, softened
115 g (4 oz/½ cup) caster (superfine) sugar
1 teaspoon natural vanilla extract
3 eggs
155 g (5½ oz/1¼ cups) self-raising flour, sifted
125 ml (4 fl oz/½ cup) milk
45 g (1⅔ oz/½ cup) desiccated coconut
½ teaspoon ground cardamom
300 g (10½ oz) sour cream
6 peaches, peeled and sliced or 2 x 410 g
    (14½ oz) tins peach slices, drained and
    patted dry
75 g (2½ oz/⅓ cup) raw (demerara) sugar

Preheat the oven to 170°C (325°F/Gas 3). Lightly grease a 16 x 26 cm (6¼ x 10½ inch) baking tin and line the base with baking paper, extending the paper over the long sides for easy removal later.

Cream the butter, caster sugar and vanilla in a large bowl using electric beaters until pale and fluffy. Add two of the eggs, one at a time, beating well after each addition. Fold in the flour and milk, in batches, alternating between the two. Fold in the coconut and cardamom. Use a spatula to spread the mixture into the prepared tin. Bake for 20 minutes, or until a skewer inserted in the centre comes out clean. Allow to cool slightly.

Meanwhile, increase the oven temperature to 200°C (400°F/Gas 6). Mix the sour cream and the remaining egg in a small bowl and spread over the cooked base. Arrange the peaches over the sour cream filling. Sprinkle with the raw sugar and bake for 30–40 minutes, or until golden and set on top. Allow to cool in the tin before slicing into fingers.

Semolina syrup slice

300 g (10½ oz/2½ cups) coarse semolina
1 teaspoon bicarbonate of soda (baking soda)
250 ml (9 fl oz/1 cup) milk
250 g (9 oz/1 cup) plain yoghurt
125 g (4½ oz/½ cup) unsalted butter, melted
2 tablespoons honey
16 blanched almonds
460 g (1 lb ¼ oz/2 cups) caster (superfine) sugar
500 ml (17 fl oz/2 cups) water
1 tablespoon lemon juice
1 tablespoon rosewater

Lightly grease a 16 x 26 cm (6¼ x 10½ inch) baking tin and line the base with baking paper, extending the paper over the long sides for easy removal later.

Place the semolina and bicarbonate of soda in a bowl and mix to combine. Whisk the milk, yoghurt, butter and honey in a separate bowl. Working quickly, stir the milk mixture into the semolina mixture until combined. Pour into the prepared tin, smooth the top with a spatula and refrigerate for 30 minutes, or until set.

Preheat the oven to 180°C (350°F/Gas 4). Score the slice diagonally into diamond shapes. Top each diamond with an almond. Bake for 25–30 minutes, or until golden brown.

Meanwhile, place the sugar and water in a saucepan. Cook, stirring occasionally, over low heat until the sugar has dissolved. Bring to the boil, reduce heat to low and simmer for 15 minutes, or until the syrup is thick. Stir in the lemon juice and rosewater and remove from the heat. Pour the syrup over the slice and allow to cool in the tin. Cut into diamonds and serve.

Peanut toffee shortbread

MAKES 18

Preheat the oven to 180°C (350°F/Gas 4). Lightly grease an 18 x 28 cm (7 x 11¼ inch) baking tin and line the base and sides with baking paper, extending the paper over the long sides for easy removal later.

Place 110 g (3¾ oz) of the butter and all the caster sugar in a large bowl and cream with electric beaters until pale and fluffy. Add the egg and beat well. Fold in the flours with a large metal spoon until just combined. Press into the prepared tin and bake for 15 minutes, or until firm and lightly coloured. Cool for 10 minutes.

Place the brown sugar, golden syrup, lemon juice and the remaining butter in a saucepan and stir over low heat until the sugar has dissolved. Simmer, stirring occasionally, for a further 5 minutes. Add the peanuts and mix well.

Spread the peanut toffee topping evenly over the base using two spoons—being careful as the mixture is very hot. Bake for 5 minutes, or until golden. Leave to slightly cool in the tin for 15 minutes, then turn out and cut into fingers while still warm.

290 g (10¼ oz) unsalted butter, softened
115 g (4 oz/½ cup) caster (superfine) sugar
1 egg
185 g (6½ oz/1½ cups) plain (all-purpose) flour, sifted
60 g (2¼ oz/½ cup) self-raising flour, sifted
185 g (6½ oz/1 cup) soft brown sugar
2 tablespoons golden syrup (light treacle)
½ teaspoon lemon juice
400 g (14 oz/2½ cups) toasted unsalted peanuts

Old English matrimonials

MAKES 15

200 g (7 oz/2 cups) quick-cooking rolled
(porridge) oats
220 g (7¾ oz/1¾ cups) plain (all-purpose) flour
230 g (8¼ oz/1¼ cups) soft brown sugar
250 g (9 oz/1 cup) unsalted butter, melted
90 g (3¼ oz/1 cup) desiccated coconut
315 g (11 oz/1 cup) strawberry jam,
slightly warmed

Preheat the oven to 180°C (350°F/Gas 4). Lightly grease a 16 x 26 cm (6¼ x 10½ inch) baking tin and line the base with baking paper, extending the paper over the long sides for easy removal later.

Combine the oats, flour, sugar, butter, salt, coconut and a pinch of salt in a large bowl. Press half the oats mixture into the prepared tin. Spread the jam on top. Sprinkle over the remaining oats mixture and press lightly with your fingertips to flatten.

Bake on the lowest shelf in the oven for 15 minutes, then transfer to the middle shelf to bake for a further 15 minutes, or until the top is golden brown. Allow to cool in the tin, then slice into pieces and serve.

Pear and walnut slice

MAKES 18

Preheat the oven to 180°C (350°F/Gas 4). Lightly grease a 20 x 30 cm (8 x 12 inch) baking tin and line the base with baking paper, extending the paper over the long sides for easy removal later.

Sift the flour, baking powder, ginger and cinnamon onto a sheet of baking paper. Beat the eggs, brown sugar, brandy and vanilla in a large bowl for 3 minutes, or until pale and creamy, then add the orange zest. Gently fold the dry ingredients into the egg mixture with a large metal spoon. Add the walnuts, pear and raisins and gently mix.

Spread the mixture into the prepared tin and smooth the top with a spatula. Bake for 35–40 minutes, or until a skewer inserted in the centre comes out clean. Cool in the tin. Slice into pieces and serve dusted with the icing sugar.

185 g (6½ oz/1½ cups) plain (all-purpose) flour
1 teaspoon baking powder
½ teaspoon ground ginger
1 teaspoon ground cinnamon
3 eggs
280 g (10 oz/1½ cups) soft brown sugar
1 teaspoon brandy
1 teaspoon natural vanilla extract
1 teaspoon finely grated orange zest
125 g (4½ oz/1 cup) walnut pieces
2 medium pears, peeled, cored and chopped
80 g (2¾ oz/½ cup) chopped raisins
icing (confectioners') sugar, sifted, for dusting

Cheese and sultana slice

125 g (4½ oz/½ cup) unsalted butter, chopped
60 g (2¼ oz/½ cup) icing (confectioners') sugar, plus extra for dusting
185 g (6½ oz/1½ cups) plain (all-purpose) flour, sifted

Topping
250 ml (9 fl oz/1 cup) milk
30 g (1 oz) unsalted butter
150 g (5½ oz/1¼ cups) crumbled soft goat's cheese
100 g (3½ oz) cream cheese, chopped
2 tablespoons caster (superfine) sugar
1 teaspoon finely grated lemon zest
60 ml (2 fl oz/¼ cup) lemon juice
30 g (1 oz/¼ cup) cornflour (cornstarch)
60 ml (2 fl oz/¼ cup) water
60 g (2¼ oz/½ cup) sultanas (golden raisins), chopped
3 egg whites
80 g (2¾ oz/⅓ cup) caster (superfine) sugar, extra

Preheat the oven to 180°C (350°F/Gas 4). Lightly grease a 20 x 30 cm (8 x 12 inch) baking tin and line the base with baking paper, extending the paper over the long sides for easy removal later.

Cream the butter and sugar in a large bowl using electric beaters until pale and fluffy. Add the flour and stir with a wooden spoon until the mixture just comes together. Press into the prepared tin. Bake for 15–20 minutes, or until golden and firm to touch. Cool.

To make the topping, combine the milk, butter, cheeses, caster sugar, lemon zest and juice in a saucepan, stirring over medium heat for 5 minutes, or until the mixture is smooth. Combine the cornflour and water in a small bowl and stir until smooth. Add to the cheese mixture and, whisking constantly, bring to the boil. Reduce the heat to low and simmer, stirring occasionally, for 3–4 minutes, or until thickened. Remove from the heat and whisk in the sultanas. Set aside. In a large bowl, whisk the egg whites until stiff peaks form. Gradually add the extra sugar, whisking well after each addition. Continue to whisk until thick and glossy, and the sugar has dissolved. Carefully fold the egg whites into the cheese mixture and mix until just combined. Spread over the cooled base. Bake for 25–30 minutes, or until golden and firm to touch. Cool completely in the tin. Use a hot knife to cut into diamonds. Dust with extra icing sugar and serve. This slice is best served on the day it is made.

Sugar and spice slice

MAKES 15

4 eggs
125 g (4½ oz/1 cup) icing (confectioners') sugar
¼ teaspoon ground cloves
¼ teaspoon ground cardamom
¼ teaspoon freshly grated nutmeg
2 teaspoons ground cinnamon
1 teaspoon finely grated lemon zest
150 g (5½ oz/1½ cups) ground almonds
100 g (3½ oz) ground hazelnuts
185 g (6½ oz/1 cup) mixed peel (mixed candied
   citrus peel)

Icing
250 g (9 oz/2 cups) icing (confectioners') sugar
1 tablespoon butter, softened
2 tablespoons dark rum
1 tablespoon hot water
30 blanched almonds, to decorate

Preheat the oven to 200°C (400°F/Gas 6). Lightly grease a 16 x 26 cm (6¼ x 10½ inch) baking tin and line the base with baking paper, extending the paper over the long sides for easy removal later.

Place the eggs and sugar in a bowl and beat with electric beaters for 5 minutes, or until frothy. Fold in the spices, lemon zest, almonds, hazelnuts, mixed peel and a pinch of salt. Pour into the prepared tin and bake for 25 minutes, or until lightly golden. Remove from the oven and allow to cool in the tin for 15 minutes, then lift onto a wire rack to cool completely.

To make the icing, sift the sugar into a large bowl and stir in the butter. Add the rum and water and mix until combined.

Cut the slice into pieces. Use a spatula to spread the icing over each piece and decorate the top with two almonds. Allow the icing to set before serving.

Apple shortcake

250 g (9 oz/2 cups) plain (all-purpose) flour
1 teaspoon baking powder
125 g (4½ oz/½ cup) unsalted butter, chilled and cut into cubes
55 g (2 oz/¼ cup) caster (superfine) sugar
1 egg, lightly beaten
1 tablespoon cold milk, plus extra, for glazing
raw (demerara) sugar, to sprinkle

Filling
4 small red apples, peeled, quartered and cored
1 teaspoon ground cinnamon
2 tablespoons caster (superfine) sugar

Preheat the oven to 180°C (350°F/Gas 4). Lightly grease a 20 cm (8 inch) square baking tin and line the base with baking paper, extending the paper over two opposite sides for easy removal later.

Sift the flour and baking powder into a large bowl. Rub in the butter with your fingertips until the mixture resembles fine breadcrumbs. Stir in the sugar. Make a well in the centre and add the combined egg and milk. Mix with a flat-bladed knife, using a cutting motion, until the mixture comes together in beads. Gently gather the mixture together and place on a lightly floured work surface. Press the dough into a ball, flatten slightly, wrap in plastic wrap and chill for 20–30 minutes.

Halve the dough. Keep half in the refrigerator and roll the other half into a 20 cm (8 inch) square. Place in the prepared tin.

To make the filling, cut the apple into thin slices. Arrange a double layer of apple in rows on the dough. Sprinkle with the combined cinnamon and sugar.

Roll the remaining pastry into a 20 cm (8 inch) square and place over the apple. Glaze with the extra milk and sprinkle with the raw sugar. Bake for 40–45 minutes, or until crisp and golden. Cut into squares and serve.

Nanaimo bars

MAKES 15

200 g (7 oz) digestive biscuits (cookies)
80 g (2¾ oz) pecans
40 g (1½ oz/⅓ cup) unsweetened cocoa powder
90 g (3¼ oz/1 cup) desiccated coconut
125 g (4½ oz/½ cup) unsalted butter, melted

Filling
60 g (2¼ oz/¼ cup) unsalted butter, softened
2 tablespoons custard powder
1 teaspoon natural vanilla extract
60 ml (2 fl oz/¼ cup) milk
250 g (9 oz/2 cups) icing (confectioners') sugar

Topping
200 g (7 oz) dark chocolate, chopped
2 teaspoons vegetable oil

Preheat the oven to 170°C (325°F/Gas 3). Lightly grease a 16 x 26 cm (6¼ x 10½ inch) baking tin and line the base with baking paper, extending the paper over the long sides for easy removal later.

Place the biscuits, pecans, cocoa and coconut in the bowl of a food processor and process until ground. Add the butter and pulse in short bursts until well combined. Press into the prepared tin. Refrigerate for 20 minutes.

To make the filling, place the butter, custard powder, vanilla, milk and sugar in the clean bowl of the food processor. Process until thick and creamy, then spread over the base.

To make the topping, place the chocolate and oil in a heatproof bowl. Half-fill a saucepan with water, bring to the boil and remove from the heat. Place the bowl over the saucepan, making sure the base of the bowl doesn't touch the water. Allow to stand, stirring occasionally, until the chocolate has melted. Use a spatula to spread the topping over the filling. Refrigerate until the chocolate has set. Cut into pieces.

Bakewell slice

125 g (4½ oz/1 cup) plain (all-purpose) flour
1 tablespoon icing (confectioners') sugar
50 g (1¾ oz) unsalted butter, chilled and cut
into cubes
1 egg yolk
2 tablespoons water

Filling

125 g (4½ oz/½ cup) butter, softened
115 g (4 oz/½ cup) caster (superfine) sugar
4 eggs
70 g (2½ oz/⅔ cup) ground almonds
2 drops of natural almond extract
160 g (5¾ oz/½ cup) raspberry jam
25 g (1 oz/¼ cup) flaked almonds

Icing

30g (1 oz/¼ cup) icing (confectioners')
sugar, sifted
2–3 teaspoons warm water

Preheat the oven to 180°C (350°F/Gas 4). Lightly grease a 20 x 30 cm (8 x 12 inch) baking tin and line the base with baking paper, extending the paper over the long sides for easy removal later.

Sift the flour and sugar into a large bowl. Rub in the butter with your fingertips until the mixture resembles fine breadcrumbs. Add the egg yolk and water and mix with a flat-bladed knife until the mixture comes together in beads. Gather into a ball, cover with plastic wrap and refrigerate for 30 minutes. Roll out between two sheets of baking paper, remove the paper and place in the prepared tin, pressing well into the edges. Bake for 10 minutes. Set aside to cool.

To make the filling, cream the butter and sugar in a bowl with electric beaters until pale and fluffy. Add the eggs, beat until well combined, and fold in the ground almonds and almond extract. Spread the jam over the pastry and pour the almond mixture on top. Smooth with a spatula and sprinkle with the flaked almonds. Bake for 30–35 minutes, or until firm. Allow to cool.

To make the icing, mix the icing sugar into a bowl with enough water to make a free-flowing paste. Drizzle the icing over the slice and leave to set. Trim the edges and cut into squares.

Classic brownies

MAKES 16

125 g (4½ oz) dark chocolate, chopped
90 g (3¼ oz/⅓ cup) unsalted butter, softened
230 g (8¼ oz/1 cup) caster (superfine) sugar
1 teaspoon natural vanilla extract
2 eggs
85 g (3 oz/⅔ cup) plain (all-purpose) flour, sifted
30 g (1 oz/¼ cup) unsweetened cocoa powder, sifted
½ teaspoon baking powder, sifted
icing (confectioners') sugar, for dusting

Preheat the oven to 180°C (350°F/Gas 4). Grease a 17 cm (6½ inch) square baking tin and line the base with baking paper, extending the paper over two opposite sides for easy removal later.

Place the chocolate in a heatproof bowl. Half-fill a saucepan with water, bring to the boil and remove from the heat. Sit the bowl over the saucepan, ensuring the base of the bowl doesn't touch the water. Stand, stirring occasionally, until the chocolate has melted. Cool slightly.

Cream the butter, caster sugar and vanilla in a medium bowl with electric beaters until pale and fluffy. Add the eggs, one at a time, beating well after each addition. Stir in the chocolate.

Fold in the combined flour, cocoa and baking powder with a metal spoon. Pour into the prepared tin and smooth the surface with a spatula. Bake for 30–35 minutes, or until firm to touch and the sides come away from the tin easily. Cool in the tin. Remove, cut into squares and serve, dusted with icing sugar.

Prune and cinnamon squares

MAKES 36

600 g (1 lb 5 oz/2¾ cups) pitted
prunes, chopped
500 ml (17 fl oz/2 cups) water
1 teaspoon bicarbonate of soda (baking soda)
125 g (4½ oz/½ cup) unsalted butter, chopped
155 g (5½ oz) soft brown sugar
2 eggs
125 g (4½ oz/1 cup) plain (all-purpose) flour
60 g (2¼ oz/½ cup) self-raising flour
½ teaspoon ground cinnamon

Cinnamon sugar
60 g (2¼ oz/½ cup) icing (confectioners') sugar
½ teaspoon ground cinnamon

Preheat the oven to 180°C (350°F/Gas 4). Grease a 23 cm (9 inch) square baking tin. Line the base with baking paper.

Combine the prunes and water in a medium saucepan, bring to the boil, then remove from the heat. Stir in the bicarbonate of soda and mix well. Cool to room temperature.

Cream the butter and sugar in a large bowl, using electric beaters, until pale and fluffy. Add the eggs, one at a time, beating well after each addition. Sift the flours and cinnamon into a separate bowl, then fold into the butter mixture alternately with the prune mixture. Spread the mixture into the prepared tin. Bake for 55–60 minutes, or until a skewer inserted in the centre comes out clean. Cool in the tin for 5 minutes, then turn out onto a wire rack to cool completely. Cut into 36 squares and place on a sheet of baking paper.

To make the cinnamon sugar, combine the sugar and cinnamon in a small bowl and mix well.

Sift the cinnamon sugar over the squares and toss gently to coat. Serve immediately (the coating will be absorbed into the squares quite quickly if left to stand).

Prune and cinnamon squares will keep (do not coat with the cinnamon sugar if you intend to store them), stored in an airtight container, for up to 4 days, or up to 3 months in the freezer.

Chewy fruit and seed slice

MAKES 18

Preheat the oven to 170°C (325°F/Gas 3). Lightly grease a 20 x 30 cm (8 x 12 inch) baking tin and line the base with baking paper, extending the paper over the long sides for easy removal later.

Place the butter and golden syrup in a small saucepan over low heat, stirring occasionally, until the butter has melted. Remove from the heat, add the peanut butter and vanilla and mix well.

Thoroughly combine the remaining ingredients in a large bowl. Make a well in the centre and pour in the butter mixture. Mix well with a large metal spoon. Press into the prepared tin and bake for 25 minutes, or until golden and firm. Allow to cool in the tin, then cut into fingers.

200 g (7 oz) unsalted butter
175 g (6 oz/½ cup) golden syrup (light treacle)
125 g (4½ oz/½ cup) crunchy peanut butter
2 teaspoons natural vanilla extract
30 g (1 oz/¼ cup) plain (all-purpose) flour
35 g (1¼ oz/⅓ cup) ground almonds
½ teaspoon mixed (pumpkin pie) spice
300 g (3 cups) quick-cooking rolled (porridge) oats
2 teaspoons finely grated orange zest
185 g (6½ oz/1 cup) soft brown sugar
45 g (1⅔ oz/½ cup) desiccated coconut
50 g (1¾ oz/⅓ cup) sesame seeds, toasted
70 g (2½ oz/½ cup) pepitas (pumpkin seeds) or shelled sunflower seeds
80 g (2¾ oz/½ cup) chopped raisins
45 g (1⅔ oz/¼ cup) mixed peel (mixed candied citrus peel)

Ginger shortbread slice

220 g (7¾ oz) unsalted butter, softened
115 g (4 oz/½ cup) caster (superfine) sugar
280 g (10 oz/2¼ cups) plain (all-purpose) flour
45 g (1⅔ oz/¼ cup) rice flour
1 tablespoon ground ginger

Topping
185 g (6½ oz/1½ cups) icing (confectioners') sugar
60 g (2¼ oz/¼ cup) unsalted butter
90 g (3¼ oz/¼ cup) golden syrup (light treacle)
2 teaspoons ground ginger
100 g (3½ oz) glacé (candied) ginger, finely chopped

Preheat the oven to 180°C (350°F/Gas 4). Lightly grease a 16 x 26 cm (6¼ x 10½ inch) baking tin and line the base and sides with baking paper, extending the paper over the long sides for easy removal later.

Cream the butter and sugar in a bowl with electric beaters until pale and fluffy. Sift the flours, ginger and a pinch of salt onto a sheet of baking paper, then fold into the butter mixture until well combined. Use a spatula to smooth the mixture into the prepared tin. Bake for 20–25 minutes, or until light golden brown. Cool slightly.

To make the topping, place the sugar, butter, golden syrup and ground ginger in a medium saucepan over low heat. Stir until the butter has melted and the mixture is smooth. Pour over the warm base and sprinkle with the glacé ginger. Allow to cool in the tin before cutting into pieces.

Nutmeg slice

Preheat the oven to 180°C (350°F/Gas 4). Lightly grease a 20 cm (8 inch) square baking tin and line the base with baking paper, extending the paper over two opposite sides for easy removal later.

Place the flour, nutmeg, cardamom, baking powder and sugar in the bowl of a food processor. Process until combined. Add the butter and pulse in short bursts until the mixture resembles breadcrumbs. Transfer 1½ cups of the mixture to the prepared tin and press down using your fingertips.

Transfer the remaining mixture to a bowl. Add the combined bicarbonate of soda and milk along with the egg and walnuts. Mix well, pour into the tin and spread evenly over the base using a spatula. Bake for 50 minutes, or until the top springs back when pressed lightly. Cover the slice with foil if the top browns too quickly. Allow to cool in the tin for 10 minutes, then lift onto a wire rack to cool completely before cutting into squares to serve.

250 g (9 oz/2 cups) plain (all-purpose) flour
2 teaspoons freshly grated nutmeg
¼ teaspoon ground cardamom
½ teaspoon baking powder
280 g (10 oz/1½ cups) soft brown sugar
125 g (4½ oz/½ cup) unsalted butter, roughly chopped
1 teaspoon bicarbonate of soda (baking soda)
185 ml (6 fl oz/¾ cup) milk
1 egg, lightly beaten
185 g (6½ oz/1½ cups) roughly chopped walnuts

Coconut rough slice

125 g (4½ oz/1 cup) self-raising flour
1 tablespoon unsweetened cocoa powder
80 g (2¾ oz/⅓ cup) caster (superfine) sugar
30 g (1 oz/⅓ cup) desiccated coconut
125 g (4½ oz/½ cup) unsalted butter, melted

Topping
185 g (6½ oz/1½ cups) icing
(confectioners') sugar
2 tablespoons unsweetened cocoa powder
1 tablespoon softened butter
90 g (3¼ oz/1 cup) desiccated coconut
160 g (5¾ oz/½ cup) condensed milk
2 teaspoons boiling water

Preheat the oven to 180°C (350°F/Gas 4). Lightly grease a 16 x 26 cm (6¼ x 10½ inch) baking tin and line the base with baking paper, extending the paper over the long sides for easy removal later.

Sift the flour and cocoa into a medium bowl. Stir in the sugar and coconut. Make a well in the centre and pour in the melted butter. Mix until thoroughly combined. Use your fingertips to press the base into the prepared tin. Bake for 20 minutes, or until lightly golden. Allow to cool completely.

To make the topping, sift the sugar and cocoa into a bowl. Stir in the butter, coconut, condensed milk and water. Use a spatula to spread the topping over the cooled base and refrigerate until set. Cut into pieces to serve.

Date and caramel shortcake

MAKES 12

125 g (4½ oz/½ cup) unsalted butter, softened
115 g (4 oz/½ cup) caster (superfine) sugar
1 teaspoon natural vanilla extract
1 egg
250 g (9 oz/2 cups) plain (all-purpose)
    flour, sifted
1 teaspoon baking powder, sifted

Filling
160 g (5¾ oz/1 cup) roughly chopped
    pitted dates
1 tablespoon soft brown sugar
2 teaspoons unsweetened cocoa powder
10 g (¼ oz) unsalted butter
250 ml (9 fl oz/1 cup) water

Preheat the oven to 180°C (350°F/Gas 4). Lightly grease an 18 x 28 cm (7 x 11¼ inch) baking tin and line the base with baking paper, extending the paper over the long sides for easy removal later.

Cream the butter, sugar and vanilla in a large bowl with electric beaters until pale and fluffy. Beat in the egg, then fold in the combined flour and baking powder, in batches, with a metal spoon. Press half the dough into the prepared tin. Form the other half into a ball, cover with plastic wrap and refrigerate for 30 minutes.

To make the filling, place the dates, sugar, cocoa, butter and water in a small saucepan. Bring to the boil, stirring, then reduce the heat to low and simmer, and continue stirring, for 12–15 minutes, or until the dates are soft and mushy and the water has been absorbed. Spread onto a plate and refrigerate to cool quickly.

Spread the filling over the pastry base with a spatula, then grate the remaining dough over the top. Bake for 35 minutes, or until golden brown and crisp. Cool in the tin for 15 minutes, then lift onto a wire rack to cool completely. Cut into fingers.

Afternoon delights

These elegant efforts are best savoured while taking
a well-deserved break.

Nectarine lattice slice

MAKES 15

250 g (9 oz/2 cups) plain (all-purpose) flour, sifted
30 g (1 oz/¼ cup) icing (confectioners') sugar
180 g (6¼ oz) unsalted butter, chilled and cut into cubes
60 g (2¼ oz/¼ cup) sour cream
icing (confectioners') sugar, for dusting

Filling
1.25 kg (2 lb 12 oz) ripe nectarines, sliced
110 g (3¾ oz/½ cup) sugar
2 tablespoons cornflour (cornstarch)
2 tablespoons Cointreau (optional)

Preheat the oven to 200°C (400°F/Gas 6). Lightly grease a 16 x 26 cm (6¼ x 10½ inch) baking tin and line the base with baking paper, extending the paper over the long sides for easy removal later.

Place the flour, sugar and a pinch of salt in the bowl of a food processor and process to combine. Add the butter and pulse in short bursts until the mixture resembles breadcrumbs. Add the sour cream and pulse until the dough just comes together.

Place the dough on a lightly floured work surface and knead gently to combine. Divide the dough in half, wrap one portion in plastic wrap and refrigerate until required. Press the other portion into the prepared tin using your fingertips. Refrigerate for 20 minutes. Transfer to the oven and bake for 15–20 minutes, or until golden.

To make the filling, combine the nectarine slices, sugar, cornflour and Cointreau, if using, in a large bowl. Allow to stand, stirring occasionally, for 15 minutes.

Meanwhile, roll out the remaining dough on a lightly floured work surface. Use a knife to cut the pastry into strips approximately 2 cm (¾ inch) wide. Pour the filling onto the cooked base and smooth the surface with a spatula. Place approximately nine strips of pastry diagonally over the filling. Repeat with another nine strips placed at right angles to the first strips, creating a lattice pattern. Bake for 40 minutes, or until browned. Set aside to cool in the tin, then lift out and slice. Serve dusted with icing sugar.

Snickerdoodle slice

MAKES 20

Preheat the oven to 180°C (350°F/Gas 4). Lightly grease a 20 x 30 cm (8 x 12 inch) baking tin and line the base with baking paper, extending the paper over the long sides for easy removal later.

Place the eggs and milk in a small bowl and whisk to combine. Sift the flour, sugar, cinnamon and baking powder into a large bowl. Make a well in the centre, pour in the egg mixture and stir with a metal spoon to roughly combine. Fold in the butter until smooth—do not overmix. Spoon half the dough into the prepared tin and smooth the surface with a spatula.

To make the cinnamon sugar, combine the sugar and cinnamon in a small bowl and mix well.

Sprinkle two-thirds of the cinnamon sugar over the dough in the tin. Gently spoon the remaining dough over the top and smooth the surface. Dust with the remaining cinnamon sugar. Bake for 25–30 minutes, or until firm. Cool in the tin for 20 minutes, then lift onto a wire rack to cool completely. Cut into pieces and serve with the cream, if desired.

2 eggs
250 ml (9 fl oz/1 cup) milk
250 g (9 oz/2 cups) plain (all-purpose) flour
230 g (8¼ oz/1 cup) caster (superfine) sugar
1 tablespoon ground cinnamon
2 teaspoons baking powder
125 g (4½ oz/½ cup) unsalted butter, melted
thick (double/heavy) cream, to serve (optional)

Cinnamon sugar
3 tablespoons sugar
3 teaspoons ground cinnamon

Rosemary and lemon syrup slice

MAKES 15

225 g (8 oz) unsalted butter, softened
1 tablespoon finely grated lemon zest
230 g (8¼ oz/1 cup) caster (superfine) sugar
1 teaspoon natural vanilla extract
3 eggs
155 g (5½ oz/1¼ cups) self-raising flour, sifted
250 g (9 oz/1 cup) sour cream
thick (double/heavy) cream, to serve (optional)

Syrup
125 ml (4 fl oz/½ cup) lemon juice
125 ml (4 fl oz/½ cup) water
230 g (8¼ oz/1 cup) caster (superfine) sugar
2 large rosemary sprigs
finely grated zest of 2 lemons

Preheat the oven to 180°C (350°F/Gas 4). Lightly grease a 16 x 26 cm (6¼ x 10½ inch) baking tin and line the base with baking paper, extending the paper over the long sides for easy removal later.

Beat the butter, lemon zest, sugar, vanilla and a pinch of salt in a large bowl with electric beaters until pale and fluffy. Add the eggs, one at a time, beating well after each addition. Gently beat in the flour and sour cream until just combined. Spread into the prepared tin. Bake for 35 minutes, or until a skewer inserted in the centre comes out clean.

Meanwhile, to make the syrup, combine the lemon juice, water, sugar, rosemary and lemon zest in a small saucepan. Cook over low heat, stirring, until the sugar dissolves. Bring to the boil, reduce the heat to low and simmer for 5 minutes, or until slightly thickened.

Use a skewer to poke small holes all over the top of the slice. Slowly pour on the hot syrup, allowing each addition to be absorbed before adding the next. Stand for 20 minutes to allow the syrup to be absorbed fully. Remove from the tin and cut into pieces. Serve topped with a dollop of cream, if desired.

Rocky road slice

MAKES 15

Lightly grease a 16 x 26 cm (6¼ x 10½ inch) baking tin and line the base with baking paper, extending the paper over the long sides for easy removal later.

Place the white chocolate in a heatproof bowl. Half-fill a saucepan with water, bring to the boil and remove from the heat. Sit the bowl over the saucepan, making sure the base of the bowl doesn't touch the water. Stand, stirring occasionally, until the chocolate has melted. Cool slightly. Pour into the prepared tin.

Sprinkle the marshmallow pieces, strawberries or Turkish delight, coconut and biscuit pieces over the chocolate base.

Melt the milk chocolate in a heatproof bowl over a saucepan of just-boiled water, making sure the base of the bowl doesn't touch the water. Cool slightly. Pour over the base and filling, then refrigerate until set. Cut into squares and serve.

400 g (14 oz) white chocolate, chopped
250 g (9 oz/2¾ cups) pink and white marshmallows, chopped
150 g (5½ oz) dried strawberries or Turkish delight, roughly chopped
45 g (1⅔ oz/¾ cup) shredded coconut, toasted
100 g (3½ oz) shortbread biscuits (cookies), roughly chopped
400 g (14 oz) milk chocolate, chopped

Orange, pistachio and semolina slice

MAKES 18

100 g (3½ oz/⅔ cup) shelled unsalted
pistachio nuts
200 g (7 oz) unsalted butter, chopped
145 g (5¼ oz/⅔ cup) caster (superfine) sugar
1 teaspoon natural vanilla extract
1 tablespoon finely grated orange zest
2 eggs
60 g (2¼ oz/½ cup) self-raising flour, sifted
125 ml (4 fl oz/½ cup) orange juice
185 g (6½ oz/1½ cups) fine semolina

Orange syrup
230 g (8¼ oz/1 cup) caster (superfine) sugar
125 ml (4 fl oz/½ cup) orange juice

Preheat the oven to 180°C (350°F/Gas 4). Lightly grease a 20 x 30 cm (8 x 12 inch) baking tin and line the base with baking paper, extending the paper over the long sides for easy removal later.

Place the pistachios on a baking tray and bake for 8–10 minutes, or until lightly toasted. Allow to cool, then chop.

Cream the butter and sugar in a medium bowl using electric beaters until pale and fluffy. Add the vanilla, orange zest and eggs, beating until combined. Fold in the flour, orange juice, semolina and pistachios with a spatula—do not overmix. Spread into the prepared tin. Bake for 30 minutes, or until golden brown and firm to touch. Cool in the tin for 10 minutes, then transfer onto a wire rack placed over a tray to catch the excess syrup.

To make the orange syrup, combine the sugar and orange juice in a small saucepan. Bring to the boil over medium heat, reduce the heat to low and simmer for 1 minute.

Spoon the orange syrup over the slice. Cool and cut into squares or diamonds and serve.

Ginger cheesecake slice

MAKES 24

200 g (7 oz) ginger-flavoured biscuits (cookies), finely crushed
60 g (2¼ oz/¼ cup) unsalted butter, melted
½ teaspoon ground cinnamon
500 g (1 lb 2 oz/2 cups) cream cheese, at room temperature
175 g (6 oz/½ cup) golden syrup (light treacle)
2 tablespoons caster (superfine) sugar
2 eggs, lightly beaten
55 g (2 oz/¼ cup) finely chopped crystallised ginger
125 ml (4 fl oz/½ cup) cream, lightly whipped

Topping
125 ml (4 fl oz/½ cup) cream
2 teaspoons caster (superfine) sugar
55 g (2 oz/¼ cup) thinly sliced crystallised ginger

Preheat the oven to 170°C (325°F/Gas 3). Lightly grease a 20 x 30 cm (8 x 12 inch) baking tin and line the base with baking paper, extending the paper over the long sides for easy removal later.

Combine the biscuits, butter and cinnamon in a bowl and mix well. Press into the prepared tin. Refrigerate for 30 minutes, or until firm.

Beat the cream cheese, golden syrup and sugar in a medium bowl using electric beaters until light and fluffy. Add the eggs, one at a time, beating well after each addition. Fold in the ginger and whipped cream. Spread over the base and bake for 25 minutes, or until just set. Turn off the oven, leave the door slightly ajar and cool in the oven. Remove from the tin when completely cool and trim the edges.

To make the topping, beat the cream and sugar in a large bowl using electric beaters until soft peaks form.

Spread the topping over the cheesecake using a spatula. Use a hot dry knife to cut the cheesecake into three strips lengthways and then cut each strip into eight pieces. Decorate with the ginger and serve.

Orange curd and meringue slice

MAKES 15

155 g (5½ oz/1¼ cups) plain (all-purpose) flour
30 g (1 oz/¼ cup) icing (confectioners') sugar
150 g (5½ oz) butter, chilled and cut into cubes
1 egg

Orange curd
170 ml (5½ fl oz/⅔ cup) freshly squeezed
  orange juice
2 teaspoons finely grated orange zest
1 tablespoon cornflour (cornstarch)
125 g (4½ oz/½ cup) unsalted butter, cut
  into cubes
230 g (8¼ oz/1 cup) caster (superfine) sugar
4 eggs, lightly beaten

Meringue
3 egg whites
115 g (4 oz/½ cup) caster (superfine) sugar

Preheat the oven to 200°C (400°F/Gas 6). Lightly grease a 16 x 26 cm (6¼ x 10½ inch) baking tin and line the base with baking paper, extending the paper over the long sides for easy removal later.

Place the flour and sugar in the bowl of a food processor and process until combined. Add the butter and pulse in short bursts until the mixture resembles fine breadcrumbs. Add the egg and pulse until the mixture just comes together. Press into the prepared tin and refrigerate for 20 minutes. Transfer to the oven and bake for 15 minutes, or until golden. Allow to cool slightly.

Meanwhile, to make the orange curd, combine the orange juice, zest and cornflour in a saucepan and stir until the cornflour has dissolved. Add the butter, sugar and eggs and place over low heat. Cook, stirring, for 5 minutes, or until the mixture thickens. Strain through a sieve into a heatproof bowl. Set aside for 5 minutes to cool slightly. Pour over the base and bake for 20 minutes, or until set.

To make the meringue, whisk the egg whites in a large bowl using electric beaters until soft peaks form. Gradually add the sugar, 1 tablespoon at a time, and beat until thick and glossy. Spoon the meringue mixture over the curd, creating peaks. Bake for 5–10 minutes, or until pale golden. Allow to cool for 15 minutes before cutting into pieces.

White chocolate crackle and lime slice

MAKES 15

300 g (10½ oz) white chocolate, chopped
175 g (6 oz) Copha (white vegetable
shortening), chopped
120 g (4¼ oz/4 cups) puffed rice cereal
125 g (4½ oz/1 cup) icing (confectioners') sugar
2 teaspoons finely grated lime zest
180 g (6¼ oz) dark chocolate, chopped

Lightly grease a 16 x 26 cm (6¼ x 10½ inch) baking tin and line the base with baking paper, extending the paper over the long sides for easy removal later.

Place the white chocolate and Copha in a saucepan. Cook, stirring frequently, over low heat until melted and combined.

Place the puffed rice, sugar and lime zest in a large bowl. Add the white chocolate mixture and stir to combine. Press into the prepared tin and smooth the surface with a spatula.

Place the dark chocolate in a heatproof bowl. Half-fill a saucepan with water, bring to the boil and remove from the heat. Sit the bowl over the saucepan, ensuring the base of the bowl doesn't touch the water. Stand, stirring occasionally, until melted. Cool slightly, then use a spoon to drizzle the chocolate over the slice. Refrigerate until set. Cut into pieces and serve.

Apricot and macaroon slice

MAKES 12

100 g (3½ oz) unsalted butter, softened
80 g (2¾ oz/⅓ cup) caster (superfine) sugar
1 egg
165 g (5¾ oz/1⅓ cups) plain (all-purpose) flour, sifted
½ teaspoon baking powder, sifted

Filling

250 g (9 oz) dried apricots, roughly chopped
1 tablespoon Grand Marnier
2 tablespoons caster (superfine) sugar
125 ml (4 fl oz/½ cup) boiling water

Topping

100 g (3½ oz) unsalted butter, softened
80 g (2¾ oz/⅓ cup) caster (superfine) sugar
1 teaspoon natural vanilla extract
2 eggs
270 g (9½ oz/3 cups) desiccated coconut
40 g (1½ oz/⅓ cup) plain (all-purpose) flour
½ teaspoon baking powder

Preheat the oven to 180°C (350°F/Gas 4). Lightly grease a 20 x 30 cm (8 x 12 inch) baking tin and line the base with baking paper, extending the paper over the long sides for easy removal later.

Cream the butter and sugar in a medium bowl using electric beaters until pale and fluffy. Add the egg and beat well. Fold in the flour and baking powder with a metal spoon. Press into the prepared tin and bake for 20–25 minutes, or until golden brown. Set aside to cool.

To make the filling, combine the apricots, Grand Marnier, sugar and water in a small bowl. Set aside for 30 minutes, then purée in a food processor. Spread evenly over the cooled base.

To make the topping, cream the butter, sugar and vanilla in a medium bowl using electric beaters until pale and fluffy. Add the eggs, one at a time, beating well after each addition. Fold in the coconut, flour and baking powder with a large metal spoon. Spoon onto the apricot filling, leaving it lumpy and loose—do not press down. Bake for 20–25 minutes, or until lightly golden. Set aside to cool completely in the tin, then slice into fingers and serve.

Earl Grey custard and sultana slice

60 g (2¼ oz/½ cup) sultanas (golden raisins)
60 ml (2 fl oz/¼ cup) Cointreau
250 ml (9 fl oz/1 cup) milk
250 ml (9 fl oz/1 cup) cream
1 vanilla bean, split lengthways and
seeds scraped
2 Earl Grey tea bags
4 egg yolks
145 g (5¼ oz/⅔ cup) caster (superfine) sugar
2 tablespoons cornflour (cornstarch)
icing (confectioners') sugar, sifted, for dusting

Base

125 g (4½ oz/½ cup) unsalted butter, softened
55 g (2 oz/¼ cup) caster (superfine) sugar
1 teaspoon finely grated orange zest
125 g (4½ oz/1 cup) plain (all-purpose) flour

Place the sultanas in a small bowl and add the Cointreau. Set aside for 30 minutes while the sultanas soak up the liqueur and soften.

Place the milk, cream, vanilla bean and vanilla seeds and the Earl Grey tea bags in a saucepan and bring to a simmer over low heat. Remove from the heat and stand, allowing the flavours to infuse for approximately 10 minutes. Then remove the vanilla bean and tea bags from the saucepan, discard, and set the milk mixture aside.

Whisk the egg yolks and sugar in a bowl until pale and thick. Whisk in the cornflour until smooth, then slowly whisk in the vanilla milk mixture. Return the contents to the cleaned saucepan and stir gently with a wooden spoon for 5 minutes, or until the custard thickens. Transfer to a bowl and fold in the sultana and liqueur mixture. Cover the surface of the custard with plastic wrap and refrigerate for 1 hour, or until cold.

Preheat the oven to 180°C (350°F/Gas 4). Lightly grease a 16 x 26 cm (6¼ x 10½ inch) baking tin and line the base with baking paper, extending the paper over the long sides for easy removal later.

Meanwhile, to make the base, cream the butter, sugar and orange zest in a bowl using electric beaters for 5 minutes, or until pale and fluffy. Fold in the flour until combined. Press the mixture into the prepared tin and refrigerate for 30 minutes.

Bake in the oven for 20 minutes, or until the base is golden. Allow to cool.

Reduce the oven temperature to 160°C (315°F/Gas 2–3).

Spread the custard over the base. Bake for 20 minutes, or until the custard is baked but has a slight wobble. Allow to cool in the tin before cutting into fingers. Serve dusted with icing sugar. (For image, see page 78.)

Rose cheesecake slice

MAKES 15

250 g (9 oz) plain sweet biscuits (cookies)
150 g (5½ oz) unsalted butter, melted
100 g (3½ oz) white chocolate, chopped
125 g (4½ oz/½ cup) cream cheese, at
room temperature
2 tablespoons caster (superfine) sugar
90 g (3¼ oz/⅓ cup) sour cream
2 teaspoons powdered gelatine
2 tablespoons boiling water
150 ml (5 fl oz) cream, lightly whipped

Rose jelly
220 g (7¾ oz/1 cup) sugar
250 ml (9 fl oz/1 cup) water
400 ml (14 fl oz) pink Champagne
2 drops of rosewater
1½ tablespoons powdered gelatine
15 edible rose petals (optional)

Preheat the oven to 170°C (325°F/Gas 3). Grease a 16 x 26 cm (6¼ x 10½ inch) baking tin and line the base with baking paper, extending the paper over the long sides for easy removal later.

Place the biscuits in the bowl of a food processor. Process until ground. Add the butter and pulse in short bursts until combined. Press the mixture into the prepared tin. Refrigerate for 20 minutes. Transfer to the oven and bake for 15 minutes, or until golden. Set aside and allow to cool.

Place the chocolate in a heatproof bowl. Half-fill a saucepan with water, bring to the boil and remove from the heat. Sit the bowl over the saucepan, ensuring the bowl doesn't touch the water. Stand, stirring occasionally, until melted. Cool slightly.

Place the cream cheese, sugar and sour cream in a bowl and beat with electric beaters until well combined and smooth.

Pour the boiling water into a small, heatproof bowl. Add the gelatine and stir until dissolved completely. Stir into the melted chocolate. Fold in the whipped cream and cream cheese mixture, spoon over the base and place in the refrigerator until set.

To make the rose jelly, place the sugar and water in a saucepan. Cook, stirring, over low heat until the sugar dissolves. Simmer, without stirring, for 5 minutes, or until reduced and syrupy. Stir in the Champagne and rosewater, sprinkle over the gelatine and whisk to combine. Pour into a bowl, refrigerate for 2 hours, or until nearly set.

Carefully spoon the rose jelly over the filling. Smooth out any lumps or bumps on the jelly's surface with a spatula and refrigerate until set.

Cut into squares and decorate each slice with one rose petal, if using. (For image, see page 79.)

Rhubarb and raspberry crumble slice

MAKES 15

Preheat the oven to 170°C (325°F/Gas 3). Lightly grease a 16 x 26 cm (6¼ x 10½ inch) baking tin and line the base with baking paper, extending the paper over the long sides for easy removal later.

Place the flour, butter and sugar in the bowl of a food processor. Process until the mixture resembles breadcrumbs. Add the egg and pulse in short bursts until just combined. Press into the prepared tin and refrigerate for 15 minutes. Transfer to the oven and bake for 15 minutes, or until pale golden. Set aside to cool.

To make the topping, place the apple, rhubarb and sugar in a medium saucepan and cook, covered, over low heat for 15 minutes, or until soft. Transfer to a bowl and allow to cool. Place the flour, butter, caster sugar and almonds in the cleaned bowl of the food processor and process to combine. Set aside 1 cup of the almond mixture. Fold the remaining mixture into the apple and rhubarb. Add the raspberries. Spoon the mixture over the base and smooth the surface with a spatula. Scatter the reserved almond filling over the top to form the crumble. Bake for 40 minutes, or until golden. Set aside to cool slightly, then lift out of the tin, cut into pieces and serve warm, if desired, with the cream.

185 g (6½ oz/1½ cups) plain (all-purpose) flour
150 g (5½ oz) unsalted butter, chilled and chopped into cubes
80 g (2¾ oz/⅓ cup) caster (superfine) sugar
1 egg
cream, to serve (optional)

Topping
2 green apples, peeled, cored and chopped
2 bunches rhubarb, about 1 kg (2 lb 4 oz) in total, washed, trimmed and chopped into 5 cm (2 inch) lengths
55 g (2 oz/¼ cup) sugar
125 g (4½ oz/1 cup) plain (all-purpose) flour
125 g (4½ oz/½ cup) unsalted butter
80 g (2¾ oz/⅓ cup) caster (superfine) sugar
200 g (7 oz/¼ cup) blanched almonds
125 g (4½ oz/1 cup) raspberries

Key lime slice

100 g (3½ oz) plain (all-purpose) flour
50 g (1¾ oz) icing (confectioners') sugar
75 g (2½ oz) unsalted butter, chilled and
chopped into cubes
icing (confectioners') sugar, sifted, for dusting
raspberries, to serve (optional)

Lime topping
4 eggs
400 g (14 oz) tin condensed milk
150 ml (5 fl oz) lime juice
1 tablespoon finely grated lime zest
50 g (1¾ oz) plain (all-purpose) flour

Preheat the oven to 180°C (350°F/Gas 4). Lightly grease an 18 x 28 cm (7 x 10¾ inch) baking tin and line the base with baking paper, extending the paper over the long sides for easy removal later.

Place the flour, sugar and butter in the bowl of a food processor and pulse in short bursts until fine and crumbly. Press into the prepared tin and bake for 12–15 minutes, or until pale golden. Remove from the oven and set aside to cool slightly.

Reduce the oven temperature to 150°C (300°F/Gas 2).

To make the lime topping, whisk the eggs and condensed milk in a medium bowl, then stir in the lime juice and zest. Sift in the flour and mix well.

Pour the lime topping over the base and bake for 30–40 minutes, or until firm. Set aside to completely cool in the tin, then cut into fingers and dust with the icing sugar. Serve with raspberries, if desired.

Choc chip pecan slice

MAKES 15

185 g (6½ oz/1½ cups) self-raising flour
95 g (3¼ oz/½ cup) soft brown sugar
125 g (4½ oz/½ cup) unsalted butter, melted and
   slightly cooled
170 g (6 oz/1 cup) chocolate chips

Topping
3 eggs, at room temperature, lightly beaten
125 g (4½ oz/⅔ cup) soft brown sugar
50 g (1¾ oz) butter, melted
175 g (6 oz/½ cup) golden syrup (light treacle)
1 teaspoon natural vanilla extract
200 g (7 oz/2 cups) pecans

Preheat the oven to 180°C (350°F/Gas 4). Lightly grease a 16 x 26 cm (6¼ x 10½ inch) baking tin and line the base with baking paper, extending the paper over the long sides for easy removal later.

Sift the flour into a large bowl. Add the sugar and mix to combine. Add the butter, mix well and fold in the chocolate chips. Press into the prepared tin and refrigerate for 20 minutes. Transfer to the oven and bake for 20 minutes, or until lightly browned. Remove from the oven and allow to cool.

To make the topping, combine the eggs, sugar, butter, golden syrup and vanilla in a bowl, mixing well. Roughly chop half the pecans and stir into the mixture.

Pour the topping over the cooled base and scatter on the remaining pecans. Bake for 30–40 minutes, or until the topping has set. Cover with foil if the nuts are browning too quickly. Allow to cool in the tin before slicing into pieces and serving.

Quince linzer slice

110 g (3¾ oz) plain (all-purpose) flour
110 g (3¾ oz) unsalted butter, chilled and
chopped into cubes
55 g (2 oz/¼ cup) caster (superfine) sugar
100 g (3½ oz/1 cup) ground almonds
¼ teaspoon ground cinnamon
1 egg yolk, lightly beaten
2 teaspoons finely grated lemon zest
1 tablespoon lemon juice
200 g (7 oz) quince jam, slightly warmed
icing (confectioners') sugar, sifted,
for dusting (optional)

Preheat the oven to 180°C (350°F/Gas 4). Lightly grease a 20 cm (8 inch) square baking tin and line the base with baking paper, extending the paper over two opposite sides for easy removal later.

Sift the flour into a large bowl. Rub the butter into the flour with your fingertips until the mixture resembles fine breadcrumbs. Stir in the sugar, ground almonds and cinnamon. Make a well in the centre and add the egg yolk, lemon zest and juice. Mix with a flat-bladed knife, using a cutting action, until the mixture comes together in beads. Gently gather together and place on a lightly floured work surface. Shape into a ball, flatten slightly, wrap in plastic wrap and chill in the refrigerator for at least 1 hour.

Lightly flour a work surface and roll out two-thirds of the pastry to fit the base of the prepared tin. Press into the tin and refrigerate for 30 minutes. Prick the base all over with a fork, then spread on the jam.

Fill a piping (icing) bag with the remaining dough and pipe a lattice pattern over the jam. Bake for 35–40 minutes, or until the pastry is golden brown. Set aside to cool slightly, then dust with the icing sugar, if desired, while still warm. Cut into pieces and serve.

Lemon squares

MAKES 30

Preheat the oven to 180°C (350°F/Gas 4). Lightly grease a 20 x 30 cm (8 x 12 inch) baking tin and line the base with baking paper, extending the paper over the long sides for easy removal later.

Cream the butter and sugar in a medium bowl using electric beaters until pale and fluffy. Fold in the flour with a metal spoon. Press into the prepared tin and bake for 20 minutes, or until golden and firm. Set aside to cool.

To make the topping, beat the eggs and sugar in a large bowl with electric beaters for 2 minutes, or until pale and thick. Stir in the lemon juice and zest. Gradually add the flour and baking powder and whisk until combined. Pour onto the base and smooth the surface with a spatula. Bake for 25 minutes, or until just firm. Cool in the tin. Dust with the icing sugar, cut into pieces and serve.

125 g (4½ oz/½ cup) unsalted butter, softened
75 g (2½ oz) caster (superfine) sugar
155 g (5½ oz/1¼ cups) plain (all-purpose) flour, sifted
icing (confectioners') sugar, sifted, for dusting

Topping
4 eggs, lightly beaten
230 g (8¼ oz/1 cup) caster (superfine) sugar
60 ml (2 fl oz/¼ cup) lemon juice
1 teaspoon finely grated lemon zest
30 g (1 oz/¼ cup) plain (all-purpose) flour, sifted
½ teaspoon baking powder, sifted

Apple and berry slice

MAKES 16

150 g (5½ oz) unsalted butter, softened
310 g (11 oz/1⅓ cups) caster (superfine) sugar
2 eggs
170 ml (5½ fl oz/⅔ cup) buttermilk
1 teaspoon natural vanilla extract
250 g (9 oz/2 cups) self-raising flour, sifted
2 large apples, peeled, cored and thinly sliced
150 g (5½ oz) blueberries
150 g (5½ oz) blackberries
icing (confectioners') sugar, sifted,
   for dusting (optional)

Preheat the oven to 180°C (350°F/Gas 4). Lightly grease a 20 x 30 cm (8 x 12 inch) baking tin and line the base with baking paper, extending the paper over the long sides for easy removal later.

Cream the butter and sugar in a large bowl using electric beaters until pale and fluffy. Add the eggs, one at a time, beating well after each addition. In a separate bowl, combine the buttermilk and vanilla. Alternately stir in the flour and the buttermilk mixture. Mix until smooth. Spread a 5 mm (¼ inch) layer in the prepared tin.

Arrange the apple on the base. Spoon the remaining mixture over the apple, smooth the surface with a spatula and scatter the berries over the top. Bake on the middle shelf in the oven for 40 minutes, or until cooked and golden. Cool in the tin for 30 minutes before lifting onto a wire rack to cool completely. Dust with the icing sugar, if using, and cut into squares.

Cider crumble slice

20 g (¾ oz) unsalted butter
1½ tablespoons golden syrup (light treacle)
150 ml (5 fl oz) alcoholic apple cider
250 g (9 oz/2 cups) self-raising flour
pinch of ground ginger
45 g (1⅔ oz/¼ cup) soft brown sugar
75 g (2½ oz) pitted dates, chopped
75 g (2½ oz/¾ cup) walnut halves, chopped
1 egg

Topping
1 large granny smith apple
40 g (1½ oz) unsalted butter
2½ tablespoons caster (superfine) sugar
60 g (2¼ oz/½ cup) plain (all-purpose) flour
75 g (2½ oz/¾ cup) walnut halves, chopped

Preheat the oven to 170°C (325°F/Gas 3). Lightly grease a 20 x 30 cm (8 x 12 inch) baking tin and line the base with baking paper, extending the paper over the long sides for easy removal later.

Melt the butter and golden syrup in a saucepan over low heat. Remove from the heat and stir in the cider.

Sift the flour and ginger into a medium bowl. Stir in the sugar, dates and walnuts. Add the golden syrup mixture and the egg and beat until smooth. Spoon into the prepared tin and smooth the surface with a spatula.

To make the topping, peel, core and thinly slice the apple, then cut into 1.5 cm (⅝ inch) pieces. Melt the butter in a small saucepan, add the sugar, flour, apple and walnuts, stirring well. Spread over the base. Bake for 30 minutes, or until golden and a skewer inserted in the centre comes out clean. Cool in the tin. Cut into pieces and serve.

Raspberry cheesecake brownies

MAKES 20

250 g (9 oz) milk chocolate, chopped
200 g (7 oz) unsalted butter, softened
185 g (6½ oz/1 cup) soft brown sugar
4 eggs
60 g (2¼ oz/½ cup) self-raising flour, sifted
30 g (1 oz/¼ cup) unsweetened cocoa
  powder, sifted
250 g (9 oz/1 cup) cream cheese,
  at room temperature
55 g (2 oz/¼ cup) caster (superfine) sugar
125 g (4½ oz/1 cup) frozen raspberries

Preheat the oven to 170°C (325°F/Gas 3). Lightly grease a 16 x 26 cm (6¼ x 10½ inch) baking tin and line the base with baking paper, extending the paper over the long sides for easy removal later.

Place the chocolate in a heatproof bowl. Half-fill a saucepan with water, bring to the boil and remove from the heat. Sit the bowl over the saucepan, ensuring the base of the bowl doesn't touch the water. Stand, stirring occasionally, until the chocolate has melted. Cool slightly.

Beat the butter and brown sugar in a large bowl using electric beaters until thick and creamy. Add three of the eggs, one at a time, beating well after each addition. Fold in the flour and cocoa. Fold in the cooled chocolate and set aside.

Clean the electric beaters and beat the cream cheese and caster sugar in a bowl until combined. Add the remaining egg and beat well. Fold in the raspberries.

Place alternate layers of the chocolate mixture and cream cheese mixture in the prepared tin. Use a skewer to swirl through the mixture to create a marbled effect. Bake for 50 minutes, or until firm. Cool completely in the tin before cutting into squares.

Jam and ricotta streusel

MAKES 15

125 g (4½ oz/1 cup) plain (all-purpose) flour
½ teaspoon baking powder
45 g (1⅔ oz/¼ cup) soft brown sugar
55 g (2 oz/½ cup) ground almonds
150 g (5½ oz) unsalted butter, chilled and
chopped into cubes
1 teaspoon natural vanilla extract
1 egg
315 g (11 oz/1 cup) apricot or jam of choice,
slightly warmed

Filling
650 g (1 lb 7 oz) ricotta cheese
80 g (2¾ oz/⅓ cup) caster (superfine) sugar
80 g (2¾ oz/½ cup) pine nuts, lightly toasted
2 tablespoons dark rum
2 eggs, lightly beaten

Lightly grease a 16 x 26 cm (6¼ x 10½ inch) baking tin and line the base with baking paper, extending the paper over the long sides for easy removal later.

Place the flour, baking powder, brown sugar, ground almonds and a pinch of salt in the bowl of a food processor. Process until combined. Add the butter and pulse in short bursts until the mixture resembles breadcrumbs. Add the vanilla and egg and pulse until the mixture just comes together. Press half of the dough into the prepared tin and refrigerate for 30 minutes. Wrap the remaining dough in plastic wrap and refrigerate until required.

Preheat the oven to 180°C (350°F/Gas 4).

Meanwhile, to make the filling, place the ricotta, sugar, pine nuts, rum and egg in a large bowl and mix well to combine.

Spread the jam over the base and cover with the ricotta filling. Crumble the remaining dough over the filling and bake for 40 minutes, or until golden. Allow to cool completely in the tin before cutting into fingers and serving.

Choc mallow bars

MAKES 15

155 g (5½ oz/1¼ cups) plain (all-purpose) flour
30 g (1 oz/¼ cup) icing (confectioners') sugar
150 g (5½ oz) unsalted butter, melted
1 egg
160 g (5¾ oz/½ cup) raspberry jam,
  slightly warmed
250 g (9 oz/2¾ cups) white marshmallows
80 ml (2½ fl oz/⅓ cup) cream
160 g (5¾ oz/1 cup) chopped unsalted peanuts
200 g (7 oz) milk chocolate, chopped
2 teaspoons vegetable oil

Preheat the oven to 200°C (400°F/Gas 6). Lightly grease a 16 x 26 cm (6¼ x 10½ inch) baking tin and line the base with baking paper, extending the paper over the long sides for easy removal later.

Sift the flour, sugar and a pinch of salt into a large bowl. Add the butter and egg, and mix well to combine. Press the dough into the prepared tin, refrigerate for 20 minutes. Transfer to the oven to bake for 20 minutes. Remove from the oven and allow to cool. Spread the jam over the base.

Place the marshmallows and cream in a saucepan. Cook, stirring occasionally, over low heat for 5 minutes, or until the marshmallows have melted. Pour over the base. Sprinkle the peanuts over the top.

Place the chocolate in a heatproof bowl. Half-fill a saucepan with water, bring to the boil and remove from the heat. Sit the bowl over the saucepan, ensuring the base of the bowl doesn't touch the water. Stand, stirring occasionally, until the chocolate has melted. Stir in the oil and cool slightly. Pour the chocolate evenly over the top of the slice and refrigerate until set. Cut into fingers and serve.

Afternoon delights

Passionfruit and lemon delicious slice

MAKES 18

125 g (4½ oz/½ cup) unsalted butter, softened
60 g (2¼ oz/½ cup) icing (confectioners')
sugar, sifted
½ teaspoon natural vanilla extract
185 g (6½ oz/1½ cups) plain (all-purpose)
flour, sifted
1 teaspoon finely grated lemon zest

Filling
100 g (3½ oz) plain (all-purpose) flour
½ teaspoon baking powder
65 g (2¼ oz/¾ cup) desiccated coconut
3 eggs
230 g (8¼ oz/1 cup) caster (superfine) sugar
170 g (6 oz) tin passionfruit pulp
2 tablespoons lemon juice
1 teaspoon finely grated lemon zest

Preheat the oven to 180°C (350°F/Gas 4). Lightly grease an 18 x 28 cm (7 x 11¼ inch) baking tin and line the base with baking paper, extending the paper over the long sides for easy removal later.

Cream the butter, sugar and vanilla in a medium bowl using electric beaters until pale and fluffy. Fold in the flour and lemon zest with a large metal spoon. Press into the prepared tin and bake for 15–20 minutes, or until lightly golden.

To make the filling, sift the flour and baking powder into a medium bowl, add the coconut and mix to combine. Lightly beat the eggs and sugar in a separate bowl, then add the passionfruit pulp, lemon juice and zest. Add the dry ingredients and mix well. Pour over the base and bake for 20 minutes, or until firm to touch. Cool in the tin. Cut into pieces and serve.

Little luxuries

Sophistication abounds with this splendid
array of sweet somethings.

Raspberry mascarpone trifle slice

375 g (13 oz) jam rollettes
60 ml (2 fl oz/¼ cup) amaretto
125 g (4½ oz) mascarpone cheese
80 g (2¾ oz/⅓ cup) caster (superfine) sugar
2 eggs, separated
200 g (7 oz) white chocolate, grated
300 g (10½ oz) raspberries
thick (double/heavy) cream, to serve (optional)

Lightly grease a 16 x 26 cm (6¼ x 10½ inch) baking tin and line the base and sides with baking paper, extending the paper over the long sides for easy removal later.

Slice each rollette into four thin rounds. Place the slices, cut side down, close together in the prepared tin. Press down lightly to ensure the base of the tin is covered. Sprinkle over the amaretto.

Place the mascarpone, sugar and egg yolks in a medium bowl and mix to combine—do not overmix.

Beat the egg whites in a separate bowl until soft peaks form. Fold the egg whites and the chocolate into the mascarpone mixture using a large metal spoon. Spread onto the base and smooth the surface with a spatula. Cover and place in the refrigerator for 2 hours, or until firm. Sprinkle on the raspberries. Cut into pieces and serve with a dollop of cream, if desired.

Rum and raisin slice

MAKES 30

Preheat the oven to 180°C (350°F/Gas 4). Lightly grease an 18 x 28 cm (7 x 11¼ inch) baking tin and line the base with baking paper, extending the paper over the long sides for easy removal later.

Combine the raisins and rum in a small bowl and set aside to soak.

Place the chocolate and butter in a heatproof bowl. Half-fill a saucepan with water, bring to the boil and remove from the heat. Sit the bowl over the saucepan, making sure the base of the bowl doesn't touch the water. Allow to stand, stirring occasionally, until melted. Stir in the sugar and cream and set aside to cool slightly.

Sift the flour into a large bowl. Add the raisin mixture, chocolate mixture and egg, mixing well. Pour into the prepared tin and smooth the surface with a spatula. Bake for 25–30 minutes, or until just set. Cool completely, then refrigerate overnight before cutting into small pieces. Dust liberally with cocoa powder and serve.

30 g (1 oz/¼ cup) raisins
80 ml (2½ fl oz/⅓ cup) dark rum
200 g (7 oz) dark chocolate, chopped
60 g (2¼ oz/¼ cup) unsalted butter, chopped
115 g (4 oz/½ cup) caster (superfine) sugar
230 ml (7¾ fl oz) thick (double/heavy) cream
125 g (4½ oz/1 cup) plain (all-purpose) flour
3 eggs, lightly beaten
unsweetened cocoa powder, sifted, for dusting

Apple tatin slice with brown sugar cream

MAKES 8

3 fuji apples, peeled
60 g (2¼ oz/¼ cup) unsalted butter, chopped
115 g (4 oz/½ cup) caster (superfine) sugar
1 sheet ready-made puff pastry

Brown sugar cream
300 ml (10½ fl oz) thick (double/heavy) cream
2 tablespoons soft brown sugar

Preheat the oven to 220°C (425°F/Gas 7). Lightly grease a 20 cm (8 inch) square baking tin and line the base and sides with baking paper, extending the paper over two opposite sides for easy removal later.

Quarter the apples and remove the cores. Cut each quarter into three wedges.

Melt the butter in a saucepan. Add the sugar and apple and cook, stirring occasionally, for 25 minutes, or until caramelised. Quickly pour into the prepared tin and spread with a spatula to cover the base.

Trim the pastry to 22 cm (8½ inches) square, place over the apple mixture, tucking the edges of the pastry down the inside of the tin and bake for 20–25 minutes, or until the pastry is golden. Allow to stand for 5 minutes before carefully turning the apple tatin out of the tin.

To make the brown sugar cream, gently whisk the cream and sugar in a small bowl until combined.

Cut the warm apple tatin into pieces and serve immediately with the brown sugar cream.

Florentine slice

MAKES 20

Preheat the oven to 180°C (350°F/Gas 4). Lightly grease a 20 x 30 cm (8 x 12 inch) baking tin and line the base and sides with baking paper, extending the paper over the long sides for easy removal later.

Combine the butter, sugar, flour, baking powder and custard powder in the bowl of a food processor and pulse in short bursts for 1 minute, or until combined. Add the water and egg yolk and pulse until the mixture resembles moist breadcrumbs. Press into the prepared tin and smooth the surface with a spatula. Bake for 20 minutes, or until lightly golden. Set aside to cool slightly.

To make the topping, place the almonds, cherries, mixed peel and cranberries in a large bowl. Melt the honey and butter in a saucepan over low heat. Whisk in the flour, then add to the fruit mixture and stir well. Pour over the base and bake for 40 minutes, or until golden. Set aside to cool in the tin. When completely cool, drizzle the melted chocolate over the top in a zigzag pattern. Once the chocolate has set, cut into pieces.

125 g (4½ oz/½ cup) unsalted butter
115 g (4 oz/½ cup) caster (superfine) sugar
155 g (5½ oz/1¼ cups) plain (all-purpose) flour, sifted
1 teaspoon baking powder
2 tablespoons custard powder
2 teaspoons water
1 egg yolk

Topping
180 g (6¼ oz/2 cups) flaked almonds
200 g (7 oz) glacé (candied) cherries
100 g (3½ oz) mixed peel (mixed candied citrus peel)
130 g (4¾ oz/1 cup) dried sweetened cranberries
350 g (12 oz/1 cup) honey
200 g (7 oz) unsalted butter
30 g (1 oz/¼ cup) plain (all-purpose) flour
30 g (1 oz) dark chocolate, melted

Cinnamon cherry slice

MAKES 18

250 g (9 oz/2 cups) self-raising flour
1 heaped teaspoon ground cinnamon
370 g (13 oz/2 cups) soft brown sugar
125 g (4½ oz/½ cup) unsalted butter, chilled
720 g (1 lb 9½ oz) jar pitted morello cherries, drained
1 teaspoon baking powder
1 egg
300 ml (10½ fl oz) cream
1 tablespoon lemon juice

Preheat the oven to 180°C (350°F/Gas 4). Lightly grease a 20 x 30 cm (8 x 12 inch) baking tin and line the base with baking paper, extending the paper over the long sides for easy removal later.

Sift the flour and cinnamon into a medium bowl and stir in the sugar. Transfer half the mixture to another bowl. Working quickly, coarsely grate the butter and divide between the bowls. Rub in the butter with your fingertips until the mixture in each bowl resembles fine breadcrumbs. Press the contents of one bowl into the prepared tin and bake for 10 minutes, or until light golden. Spread the cherries evenly over the base.

Add the baking powder to the reserved flour mixture and mix well. Lightly whisk the egg, cream and lemon juice in a separate bowl and add the flour mixture, stirring well with a large metal spoon. Spread over the cherries and bake for 40 minutes, or until a skewer inserted in the centre comes out clean. Allow to cool in the tin, then cut into pieces.

Dulce de leche slice

Caramel
2 x 400 g (14 oz) tins condensed milk
2 tablespoons dark rum
50 g (1¾ oz) unsalted butter

185 g (6½ oz/1 cup) soft brown sugar
220 g (7¾ oz/1¾ cups) plain (all-purpose) flour
45 g (1⅔ oz/½ cup) desiccated coconut
1 teaspoon baking powder
1 egg
1 teaspoon natural vanilla extract
180 g (6¼ oz) unsalted butter
200 g (7 oz) milk chocolate, chopped
20 g (¾ oz) Copha (white vegetable shortening), chopped

To make the caramel, combine the condensed milk, rum and butter in a saucepan. Cook over low–medium heat, stirring constantly, for 15 minutes, or until a light caramel colour. Remove from the heat and set aside.

Preheat the oven to 200°C (400°F/Gas 6). Lightly grease a 16 x 26 cm (6¼ x 10½ inch) baking tin and line the base and sides with baking paper, extending the paper over the long sides for easy removal later.

Place the sugar, flour, coconut, baking powder, egg and vanilla in the bowl of a food processor and pulse in short bursts to combine. Place the butter in a saucepan and cook over medium heat for 6–8 minutes, or until light brown and nutty. Quickly add to the flour mixture and process until just combined. Press half the flour mixture into the prepared tin. Pour on the caramel, then sprinkle over the remaining flour mixture. Bake on the lowest shelf of the oven for 10 minutes. Transfer to a higher shelf and bake for 10–15 minutes, until golden. Allow to cool in the tin.

Place the chocolate and Copha in a heatproof bowl over a saucepan of simmering water, making sure the base of the bowl doesn't touch the water. Cook, stirring occasionally, until the chocolate has melted. Spread over the slice. Refrigerate until the chocolate has set. Cut into pieces and serve.

Cardamom and almond barfi

MAKES 15

450 g (1 lb) blanched almonds, toasted
150 g (5½ oz/1½ cups) powdered milk
½ teaspoon ground cardamom
50 g (1¾ oz) butter, chopped into cubes
230 g (8¼ oz/1 cup) caster (superfine) sugar
250 ml (9 fl oz/1 cup) water
gold leaf or cachous (optional)

Lightly grease a 16 x 26 cm (6¼ x 10½ inch) baking tin and line the base with baking paper, extending the paper over the long sides for easy removal later.

Place the almonds in the bowl of a food processor and process until ground. Transfer to a large bowl. Add the powdered milk, cardamom and butter and mix until well combined.

Combine the sugar and water in a small saucepan and stir over low heat until the sugar has dissolved. Allow to simmer, without stirring, for 5 minutes, or until reduced and syrupy. Quickly pour onto the almond mixture and stir well. Transfer to the prepared tin, smooth the surface with a spatula and scatter over the gold leaf or cachous, if using. Refrigerate until firm. Cut into pieces and serve.

White chocolate mousse slice

MAKES 15

Lightly grease a 16 x 26 cm (6¼ x 10½ inch) baking tin and line the base and sides with baking paper.

Place the biscuits and ground almonds in the bowl of a food processor and process to combine. Pour in the butter and pulse in short bursts until the mixture just comes together. Press into the prepared tin and refrigerate for 30 minutes.

Place the chocolate, cream and vanilla extract in a small saucepan and stir over low heat until melted and smooth. Dissolve the gelatine in the hot water and add to the chocolate mixture. Whisk the egg yolks into the chocolate mixture and transfer to a large bowl. Set aside to cool.

Beat the egg whites in a bowl using electric beaters until soft peaks form. Fold the whipped cream into the cooled chocolate mixture, then fold in the egg whites, in two batches. Spread over the prepared base. Cover and refrigerate for 4 hours or overnight.

Meanwhile, to make the plum compote, combine the wine, water, sugar and vanilla seeds in a saucepan and cook, stirring, over low heat until the sugar has dissolved. Simmer for 10 minutes, without stirring, or until reduced by half. Remove from the heat, stir in the plums and transfer to a bowl. Allow to cool. Cover and refrigerate for 4 hours or overnight. Cut into squares and serve with the plum compote.

250 g (9 oz) plain sweet biscuits (cookies), roughly crushed
70 g (2½ oz/⅔ cup) ground almonds
150 g (5½ oz) unsalted butter, melted
200 g (7 oz) white chocolate, chopped
60 ml (2 fl oz/¼ cup) cream
1 teaspoon natural vanilla extract
1 teaspoon powdered gelatine
1 tablespoon hot water
2 eggs, separated
125 ml (4 fl oz/½ cup) cream, lightly whipped

Plum compote
250 ml (9 fl oz/1 cup) red wine
250 ml (9 fl oz/1 cup) water
220 g (7¾ oz/1 cup) sugar
1 vanilla bean, split lengthways and seeds scraped
1 kg (2 lb 4 oz) plums, cut into wedges

Passionfruit bougatsa slice

MAKES 12

250 ml (9 fl oz/1 cup) milk
250 ml (9 fl oz/1 cup) cream (whipping)
1 vanilla bean, split lengthways and
seeds scraped
2 eggs
285 g (10 oz/1¼ cups) caster (superfine) sugar
85 g (3 oz/⅔ cup) fine semolina
125 ml (4 fl oz/½ cup) passionfruit pulp (about
4 large passionfruit)
16 sheets filo pastry
200 g (7 oz) unsalted butter, melted
440 g (15½ oz/2 cups) sugar
500 ml (17 fl oz/2 cups) water
90 g (3¼ oz/¼ cup) honey
3 large strips lemon zest, white pith removed
80 ml (2½ fl oz/⅓ cup) lemon juice
2 tablespoons passionfruit pulp (about 1 large
passionfruit), extra
vanilla ice cream, to serve

Place the milk, cream, vanilla bean and seeds in a large saucepan over low heat and bring to a simmer. Remove from the heat and allow to infuse for 10 minutes. Remove the vanilla bean.

Meanwhile, whisk the eggs and caster sugar in a bowl until smooth. Gradually whisk in the cream mixture, then pour the combined mixtures into the cleaned saucepan. Add the semolina and whisk over medium heat for 2–3 minutes, or until thickened. Stir in the ½ cup passionfruit pulp and set aside to cool. Cover and refrigerate until completely chilled.

Preheat the oven to 200°C (400°F/Gas 6). Lightly grease a 16 x 26 cm (6¼ x 10½ inch) baking tin.

Place one filo sheet on a clean work surface and brush with a little of the melted butter. Top with another sheet and brush with melted butter. Repeat this process with six more sheets of pastry. Fold the filo stack in half crossways, place in the base of the prepared tin and spoon on the custard.

Repeat layering the remaining filo sheets, brushing each with the butter. Fold in half crossways and place on top of the custard. Use a small sharp knife to score a diamond pattern on top of the pastry. Brush with the remaining butter. Bake for 30 minutes, or until golden. Set aside for 5 minutes to cool slightly.

Combine the sugar, water, honey and lemon zest and juice in a medium saucepan. Stir over low heat until the sugar has dissolved. Bring to the boil and cook for 5–7 minutes, or until reduced by half. Remove the lemon zest and allow to cool.

Spoon half the cooled syrup over the hot pastry, allowing it to soak in. Set aside to cool, then cover with plastic wrap and refrigerate overnight. Place the remaining sugar syrup in a bowl. Cover and refrigerate overnight.

The next day, preheat the oven to 160°C (315°F/ Gas 2–3). Place the bougatsa in the oven and cook for 15 minutes, or until slightly warmed.

Place the reserved sugar syrup in a small saucepan and bring to a simmer. Remove from the heat and stir in the extra passionfruit pulp.

Cut the bougatsa into pieces and serve with the ice cream drizzled with the passionfruit syrup. (For image, see 128.)

Chestnut cream slice

Chocolate sponges

80 g (2¾ oz) self-raising flour
60 g (2¼ oz/½ cup) plain (all-purpose) flour
1 tablespoon unsweetened cocoa powder
110 g (3¾ oz) caster (superfine) sugar
2 eggs, lightly beaten
2 teaspoons natural vanilla extract
120 g (4¼ oz/½ cup) unsalted butter, softened
125 ml (4 fl oz/½ cup) milk
125 ml (4 fl oz/½ cup) brandy

Base

60 g (2¼ oz/½ cup) plain (all-purpose) flour
2 tablespoons unsweetened cocoa powder
2 tablespoons caster (superfine) sugar
60 g (2¼ oz/¼ cup) unsalted butter, melted
1 tablespoon milk
½ teaspoon natural vanilla extract

Preheat the oven to 180°C (350°F/Gas 4). Grease two 17 cm (6½ inch) square baking tins and line the bases and sides with baking paper.

To make the chocolate sponges, sift the flours and the cocoa into a large bowl, stir in the sugar and make a well in the centre. Combine the egg, vanilla, butter and milk in a separate bowl, pour into the well and stir until just combined. Divide evenly between the prepared tins and bake for 10–15 minutes, or until the top springs back on each cake when lightly touched. Set aside to cool for 5 minutes, then turn out onto wire racks to cool completely. Brush the top of each cake with the brandy.

Increase the oven temperature to 190°C (375°F/Gas 5). Lightly grease a 17 cm (6½ inch) square baking tin and line the base with baking paper, extending the paper over two opposite sides for easy removal later.

To make the base, sift the flour, cocoa and sugar into a bowl. Add the butter, milk and vanilla and mix until well combined. Press into the prepared tin and smooth the top with the back of a spoon. Refrigerate for 20 minutes. Cover the dough with baking paper, fill with baking beads or uncooked rice and bake for 10–15 minutes, or until dry. Remove the paper and weights. Reduce the oven temperature to 180°C (350°F/Gas 4) and bake for 8–10 minutes, or until deep brown. Leave to cool.

To make the chestnut cream, beat the butter, chestnut purée, sugar and brandy in a bowl using electric beaters until smooth.

Spread half the chestnut cream over the cooled base and place one layer of chocolate sponge on top, pressing down gently. Repeat with the remaining chestnut cream and chocolate sponge.

To make the chocolate glaze, place the chocolate, butter and cream in a heatproof bowl. Half-fill a saucepan with water, bring to the boil and remove from the heat. Sit the bowl over the saucepan, making sure the base of the bowl doesn't touch the water. Allow to stand, stirring occasionally, until the chocolate and butter have melted. Stir until smooth and well combined. Set aside to cool.

Spread the chocolate glaze over the slice and leave to set. Cut into pieces and serve. (For image, see page 129.)

Chestnut cream
30 g (1 oz) unsalted butter, softened
250 g (9 oz/1 cup) unsweetened chestnut purée
60 g (2¼ oz/½ cup) icing (confectioners') sugar
2 tablespoons brandy

Chocolate glaze
100 g (3½ oz) dark chocolate, chopped
60 g (2¼ oz/¼ cup) unsalted butter, chopped
1 tablespoon cream

Peppermint chocolate slice

MAKES 20

Preheat the oven to 180°C (350°F/Gas 4). Grease a 20 x 30 cm (8 x 12 inch) baking tin and line the base with baking paper, extending the paper over the long sides for easy removal later.

Sift the flour and baking powder into a bowl and add the brown sugar. Stir in the melted butter and press into the prepared tin. Bake for 20 minutes, or until lightly golden. Set aside to cool.

Melt the Copha in a small saucepan over medium heat. Add the icing sugar, peppermint extract, milk and cream, mix well and pour over the base. Leave to set.

To make the chocolate topping, place the chocolate and butter in a heatproof bowl. Half-fill a saucepan with water, bring to the boil and remove from the heat. Sit the bowl over the saucepan, making sure the base of the bowl doesn't touch the water. Stand, stirring occasionally, until melted and smooth. Cool slightly.

Spread the chocolate topping over the peppermint filling and smooth with a spatula. Transfer to the refrigerator to chill until set. Cut into pieces and serve.

220 g (7¾ oz/1¾ cups) plain (all-purpose) flour
1 teaspoon baking powder
95 g (3¼ oz/½ cup) soft brown sugar
180 g (6¼ oz) unsalted butter, melted
60 g (2¼ oz) Copha (white vegetable shortening)
435 g (15¼ oz/3½ cups) icing (confectioners') sugar, sifted
1 teaspoon natural peppermint extract
2 tablespoons milk
2 tablespoons cream

Chocolate topping
300 g (10½ oz) dark chocolate, chopped
70 g (2½ oz) unsalted butter, chopped

Angel food slice with white balsamic strawberries

MAKES 12

45 g (1⅔ oz/½ cup) flaked almonds
90 g (3¼ oz/¾ cup) plain (all-purpose) flour
6 egg whites
pinch of salt
1 teaspoon cream of tartar
170 g (6 oz/¾ cup) caster (superfine) sugar
1 teaspoon natural vanilla extract
2 tablespoons amaretto
thick (double/heavy) cream, to serve (optional)

White balsamic strawberries
500 g (1 lb 2 oz/3⅓ cups) strawberries, hulled and halved
60 ml (2 fl oz/¼ cup) white balsamic vinegar
2 tablespoons caster (superfine) sugar

Preheat the oven to 180°C (350°F/Gas 4). Lightly grease a 16 x 26 cm (6¼ x 10½ inch) baking tin and line the base and sides with baking paper, extending the paper over the long sides for easy removal later. Sprinkle the almonds over the base of the tin.

Sift the flour into a bowl. Sift again. Repeat this process four or five times. Combine the egg whites and salt in a separate bowl and beat until soft peaks form. Add the cream of tartar and continue beating until firm peaks form. Gradually add the sugar and beat until thick and glossy. Gently fold in the vanilla, flour and amaretto with a large metal spoon. Do not overmix and lose the volume of the egg whites. Pour into the prepared tin and bake for 40 minutes, or until lightly golden. Allow to cool slightly.

To make the white balsamic strawberries, place the strawberries in a large non-metallic dish. Add the vinegar and sugar and stir well, making sure the strawberries are evenly coated.

Remove the slice from the tin, cut into pieces and serve topped with some of the strawberries and a dollop of cream, if desired.

Choc cherry slice

MAKES 28

Preheat the oven to 180°C (350°F/Gas 4). Lightly grease an 18 x 28 cm (7 x 10¾ inch) baking tin and line the base with baking paper, extending the paper over the long sides for easy removal later.

Sift the flour, cocoa and sugar into a medium bowl, add the butter and vanilla and mix to form a dough. Gather together and turn out onto a well-floured work surface. Gently knead for 1 minute, then press into the base of the prepared tin. Place in the refrigerator to chill for 20 minutes. Cover with baking paper and baking beads or uncooked rice and bake for 10–15 minutes, or until pale golden. Remove the paper and weights and bake for 5 minutes, or until golden. Set aside to cool.

To make the filling, combine the cherries, sugar and coconut in a medium bowl. Stir in the condensed milk, butter and Copha. Spread the filling over the cooled base, then transfer to the refrigerator to chill for 30 minutes.

To make the chocolate topping, place the chocolate and butter in a heatproof bowl. Half-fill a saucepan with water, bring to the boil and remove from the heat. Sit the bowl over the saucepan, making sure the base of the bowl doesn't touch the water. Allow to stand, stirring occasionally, until melted. Pour over the cooled cherry filling and smooth with a spatula. Stand at room temperature for 15 minutes before cutting into squares.

125 g (4½ oz/1 cup) plain (all-purpose) flour
40 g (1½ oz/⅓ cup) unsweetened cocoa powder
80 g (2¾ oz/⅓ cup) caster (superfine) sugar
125 g (4½ oz/½ cup) unsalted butter, melted
1 teaspoon natural vanilla extract

Filling
420 g (15 oz/2 cups) glacé (candied) cherries, finely chopped
60 g (2¼ oz/½ cup) icing (confectioners') sugar
135 g (4¾ oz/1½ cups) desiccated coconut
160 g (5¾ oz/½ cup) condensed milk
60 g (2¼ oz/¼ cup) unsalted butter, melted
25 g (1 oz) Copha (white vegetable shortening), melted

Chocolate topping
150 g (5½ oz) dark chocolate, chopped
25 g (1 oz) unsalted butter, chopped

Hazelnut meringue and chocolate layer slice

MAKES 18

100 g (3½ oz/¾ cup) hazelnuts, lightly toasted
and skinned
30 g (1 oz/¼ cup) cornflour (cornstarch)
40 g (1½ oz/⅓ cup) icing (confectioners') sugar
5 egg whites
200 g (7 oz) caster (superfine) sugar
unsweetened cocoa powder, sifted, for dusting

Ganache
250 g (9 oz) dark chocolate, chopped
125 ml (4 fl oz/½ cup) cream
2 tablespoons Frangelico

Preheat the oven to 170°C (325°F/Gas 3). Lightly grease two 26 x 38 cm (10½ x 15 inch) baking trays and line with baking paper.

Place the hazelnuts, cornflour and icing sugar in the bowl of a food processor and process in short bursts until the mixture resembles coarse breadcrumbs.

Beat the egg whites in a large bowl using electric beaters until soft peaks form. Gradually add the caster sugar and beat until thick and glossy. Lightly fold the egg whites into the hazelnut mixture.

Divide the mixture evenly between the two trays and smooth the surface with a spatula. Bake for 30 minutes, or until light golden.

Trim the edges and cut a 26 cm (10½ inch) square from each meringue, reserving the trimmings. Allow to cool completely.

To make the ganache, place the chocolate, cream and Frangelico in a heatproof bowl. Half-fill a saucepan with water, bring to the boil and remove from the heat. Sit the bowl over the saucepan, making sure the base of the bowl doesn't touch the water. Allow to stand, stirring occasionally, until the chocolate has just melted. Stir until smooth. Cover the surface with plastic wrap and leave to cool completely, stirring occasionally.

Line a 26 cm (10½ inch) square baking tin with baking paper, extending the paper over two opposite sides for easy removal later. Line the base with one meringue square and carefully spread on half the ganache. Place the reserved meringue trimmings side by side over the ganache, then smooth the remaining ganache over the top. Finish with the remaining meringue square, press down gently and refrigerate for 1 hour.

Remove the slice from the refrigerator. Dust with the cocoa and cut into thin fingers with a serrated knife.

NOTES: Toast the hazelnuts in a 180°C (350°F/Gas 4) oven for 5–10 minutes, or until lightly golden. Tip the nuts onto a clean tea towel (dish towel) and rub gently to remove the skins.

Don't worry if the pieces of meringue break up a little, the ganache will adhere to the pieces when it sets. (For image, see page 140.)

Pineapple upside-down slice

100 g (3½ oz) unsalted butter, roughly chopped
140 g (5 oz/¾ cup) soft brown sugar
250 g (9 oz pineapple), core removed, chopped into 5 mm (¼ inch) slices
thick (double/heavy) cream, to serve (optional)

Topping
200 g (7 oz) unsalted butter, softened
230 g (8¼ oz/1 cup) caster (superfine) sugar
3 eggs
185 g (6½ oz/1½ cups) plain (all-purpose) flour, sifted
1½ teaspoons baking powder, sifted
1 tablespoon freshly grated ginger
250 ml (9 fl oz/1 cup) buttermilk

Preheat the oven to 180°C (350°F/Gas 4). Lightly grease a 16 x 26 cm (6¼ x 10½ inch) baking tin and line the base and sides with baking paper, extending the paper over the long sides for easy removal later.

Scatter the butter over the base of the prepared tin. Sprinkle on the sugar and arrange the pineapple on top.

To make the topping, cream the butter and sugar in a bowl using electric beaters until pale and fluffy. Add the eggs, one at a time, beating well after each addition. Fold in the flour, baking powder and ginger alternately with the buttermilk. Spoon the mixture over the base. Bake for 45–50 minutes or until a skewer inserted in the centre comes out clean.

Allow to cool for 10 minutes and, while still warm, turn out onto a cutting board, cut into pieces and serve with a dollop of cream, if desired.

Truffle macaroon slice

MAKES 24

3 egg whites
170 g (6 oz/¾ cup) caster (superfine) sugar
180 g (6¼ oz/2 cups) desiccated coconut
250 g (9 oz) dark chocolate, chopped
300 ml (10½ fl oz) cream
1 tablespoon unsweetened cocoa powder, sifted,
  for dusting

Preheat the oven to 180°C (350°F/Gas 4). Lightly grease a 20 x 30 cm (8 x 12 inch) baking tin and line the base with baking paper, extending the paper over the long sides for easy removal later.

Beat the egg whites in a large bowl until soft peaks form. Gradually add the sugar, beating well after each addition until stiff and glossy. Fold in the coconut. Spread into the prepared tin and bake for 20 minutes, or until pale golden brown. While still warm, lightly but firmly press down into the tin with a spatula. Cool completely.

Place the chocolate in a heatproof bowl. Half-fill a saucepan with water, bring to the boil, then remove from the heat. Sit the bowl over the saucepan, making sure the base of the bowl doesn't touch the water. Stand, stirring occasionally, until the chocolate has melted. Cool slightly.

Beat the cream until soft peaks form. Gently fold in the melted chocolate until well combined—do not overmix or it will curdle. Spread evenly over the macaroon base and refrigerate for 3 hours, or until set. Remove from the tin, dust with the cocoa and cut into fingers.

Chocolate caramel slice

200 g (7 oz) plain chocolate biscuits
(cookies), crushed
100 g (3½ oz) unsalted butter, melted
2 tablespoons desiccated coconut

Caramel layer
125 g (4½ oz/½ cup) unsalted butter
400 g (14 oz) tin condensed milk
80 g (2¾ oz/⅓ cup) caster (superfine) sugar
3 tablespoons maple syrup

Chocolate layer
250 g (9 oz) dark chocolate, chopped
2 teaspoons vegetable oil

Grease a 20 x 30 cm (8 x 12 inch) baking tin and line the base and sides with baking paper, extending the paper over the long sides for easy removal later.

Combine the biscuits, butter and coconut in a bowl, press evenly into the prepared tin and smooth the surface with a spatula.

To make the caramel layer, combine the butter, condensed milk, sugar and maple syrup in a small saucepan. Stir over low heat for 15 minutes, or until the sugar has dissolved and the mixture is smooth, thick and lightly coloured. Remove from the heat and cool slightly. Pour over the biscuit base and smooth the surface with a spatula. Refrigerate for 30 minutes, or until firm.

To make the chocolate layer, place the chocolate in a heatproof bowl. Half-fill a saucepan with water, bring to the boil and remove from the heat. Sit the bowl over the saucepan, making sure the base of the bowl doesn't touch the water. Allow to stand, stirring occasionally, until the chocolate has melted. Add the oil and stir until smooth.

Spread the chocolate layer over the caramel and leave until partially set before marking into 12 triangles. Refrigerate until set. Cut into triangles using a hot, wet knife before serving. This slice will keep, stored in an airtight container, for up to 2 days.

Fig and frangipane slice

MAKES 8

165 g (5¾ oz/1⅓ cups) plain (all-purpose) flour
2 tablespoons caster (superfine) sugar
pinch of salt
125 g (4½ oz/½ cup) unsalted butter, chilled and
   cut into cubes
1 egg
icing (confectioners') sugar, sifted, for dusting

Topping
115 g (4 oz) unsalted butter, softened
85 g (3 oz) caster (superfine) sugar
150 g (5½ oz/1½ cups) ground almonds
1 egg
1 tablespoon plain (all-purpose) flour
2 tablespoons Frangelico
3 fresh large figs, cut into quarters

Preheat the oven to 200°C (400°F/Gas 6). Lightly grease a 10 x 33 cm (4 x 13 inch) baking tin and line the base and sides with baking paper, extending the paper over the long sides for easy removal later.

Place the flour, sugar and salt in the bowl of a food processor. Process until combined. Add the butter and pulse in short bursts until the mixture resembles breadcrumbs. Add the egg and process until the mixture just comes together in a ball. Press into the prepared tin. Refrigerate for 20 minutes. Transfer to the oven and bake for 20 minutes, or until golden. Remove and allow to cool.

Reduce the oven temperature to 180°C (350°F/Gas 4).

To make the topping, place the butter, sugar, ground almonds, egg, flour and Frangelico in a bowl and mix well to combine. Spread the almond mixture over the base using a spatula. Then gently press the figs into the almond mixture. Bake for 30–40 minutes, or until set. Set aside to cool in the tin, then turn out and slice. Serve dusted with the icing sugar.

Panettone pudding slice

MAKES 8

450 g (1 lb) panettone
50 g (1¾ oz) unsalted butter, softened
160 g (5¾ oz/½ cup) strawberry jam
300 ml (10½ fl oz) milk
3 eggs, lightly beaten
55 g (2 oz/¼ cup) caster (superfine) sugar
60 ml (2 fl oz/¼ cup) Frangelico
2 tablespoons raw (demerara) sugar

Marsala cream
250 ml (9 fl oz/1 cup) cream (whipping)
2 tablespoons sweet Marsala
2 tablespoons icing (confectioners') sugar

Preheat the oven to 160°C (315°F/Gas 2–3). Lightly grease a 16 x 26 cm (6¼ x 10½ inch) baking tin and line the base and sides with baking paper, extending the paper over the long sides for easy removal later. Preheat the grill (broiler) to high.

Cut the panettone into six thick slices and grill for 2 minutes on each side, or until golden. Butter each slice, spread with the jam and roughly chop into 3 cm (1¼ inch) pieces. Place the panettone pieces in the prepared tin.

Combine the milk, eggs, caster sugar and Frangelico in a medium bowl and whisk well. Pour over the panettone and set aside for 20 minutes to allow the custard to be absorbed. Sprinkle with the raw sugar and bake for 40 minutes, or until the custard is set and the top is golden. Set aside to cool slightly. To make the Marsala cream, combine the cream, Marsala and sugar in a bowl and mix well. Cover with plastic wrap and refrigerate until required.

Cut the slice into pieces while still warm. Serve with the Marsala cream.

Pear and star anise tarte fine slice

MAKES 6

185 ml (6 fl oz/¾ cup) port
125 g (4 fl oz/½ cup) caster (superfine) sugar
500 ml (17 fl oz/2 cups) water
2 star anise
3 firm beurre bosc pears, peeled, halved
  and cored
1 sheet ready-rolled puff pastry
thick (double/heavy) cream or vanilla ice cream,
  to serve (optional)

Combine the port, sugar, water, star anise and pears in a large saucepan over low heat and bring to a simmer, stirring occasionally. Cover and cook for 20 minutes, or until the pears are tender (the cooking time will depend on the ripeness of the pears). Remove from the heat and allow the pears to cool in the syrup.

Preheat the oven to 220°C (425°F/Gas 7). Lightly grease a 16 x 26 cm (6¼ x 10½ inch) baking tin and line the base and sides with baking paper, extending the paper over the long sides for easy removal later.

Lightly flour a work surface and roll out the pastry. Trim and press into the prepared tin. Cover with another baking tin the same size and bake for 10 minutes, or until the edges of the pastry are cooked through but not browned.

Remove the pears, reserving the poaching syrup. Place the reserved poaching syrup in a saucepan and simmer over medium heat for 25 minutes, or until reduced and syrupy.

Meanwhile, slice the pears thinly, without slicing through to the top and arrange on the pastry. Bake for 20–25 minutes, or until the pears are warmed through and the pastry is golden and crisp. Serve with the syrup and cream or ice cream, if desired.

Cassata slice

MAKES 16

Cake

125 g (4½ oz) dark chocolate, chopped
125 g (4½ oz/½ cup) unsalted butter, chopped
230 g (8¼ oz/1 cup) caster (superfine) sugar
3 eggs, lightly beaten
1 teaspoon natural vanilla extract
125 g (4½ oz/1 cup) plain (all-purpose) flour, sifted
30 g (1 oz/¼ cup) unsweetened cocoa powder, sifted
2½ tablespoons Grand Marnier
icing (confectioners') sugar, sifted, for dusting

Filling

250 g (9 oz/1 cup) ricotta cheese
80 ml (2½ fl oz/⅓ cup) thick (double/heavy) cream
30 g (1 oz) caster (superfine) sugar
60 ml (2 fl oz/¼ cup) Grand Marnier
4 tablespoons coarsely chopped mixed glacé (candied) fruit (such as cherries, mixed peel, figs and cedro)
80 g (2¾ oz) dark (semisweet) chocolate, coarsely chopped
50 g (1¾ oz/⅓ cup) roasted whole almonds, roughly chopped

Preheat the oven to 180°C (350°F/Gas 4). Grease a 17 cm (6½ inch) square baking tin and line the base and sides with foil, extending the foil over two opposite sides for easy removal later.

To make the cake, place the chocolate and butter in a heatproof bowl. Half-fill a saucepan with water, bring to the boil and remove from the heat. Sit the bowl over the saucepan, making sure the base doesn't touch the water. Allow to stand, stirring occasionally, until the chocolate and butter have melted. Cool slightly, then whisk in the caster sugar, egg and vanilla. Fold in the flour and cocoa, pour into the prepared tin and smooth the surface with a spatula. Bake for 30 minutes, or until firm to touch. Allow to cool.

To make the filling, combine the ingredients in a large bowl and mix well. Cover and refrigerate until needed.

Cut the cake in half horizontally. Brush the cut sides with the Grand Marnier. Place the bottom layer of the cake, cut side up, in the prepared tin. Spread on the filling and smooth the surface. Place the remaining cake layer on top, cut side down, and press firmly. Cover and refrigerate for at least 1 hour. Trim, cut into squares and dust with the icing sugar.

Index

Published in 2009 by Murdoch Books Pty Limited

Murdoch Books Australia
Pier 8/9
23 Hickson Road
Millers Point NSW 2000
Phone: +61 (0) 2 8220 2000
Fax: +61 (0) 2 8220 2558
www.murdochbooks.com.au

Murdoch Books UK Limited
Erico House, 6th Floor
93–99 Upper Richmond Road
Putney, London SW15 2TG
Phone: +44 (0) 20 8785 5995
Fax: +44 (0) 20 8785 5985
www.murdochbooks.co.uk

Publisher: Jane Lawson
Project manager: Jane Massam
Editor: Megan Johnston
Food editor: Chrissy Freer
Design concept: Reuben Crossman
Design layout: Helen Beard
Photographer: Brett Stevens
Stylist: Lynsey Fryers
Food preparation: Wendy Quisumbing, Hannah Dodds,
Tracey Meharg
Recipes by: Alison Adams and the Murdoch Books
test kitchen
Production: Kita George

National Library of Australia Cataloguing-in-Publication Data
Title: Indulgence Slices: a fine selection of sweet treats
ISBN: 9781741961195 (hbk)
Series: Indulgence series.
Notes: Includes index.
Subjects: Bars (Desserts)
Dewey Number: 641.865

A catalogue record for this book is available from the
British Library.

Colour separation by SPLITTING IMAGE

PRINTED IN CHINA.

The Publisher and stylist would like to thank Resene Paints,
Porters Paints, Tibet Gallery, Living Edge, Spence and Lyda
and Miljo for lending equipment for use and photography.

IMPORTANT: Those who might be at risk from the effects of
salmonella poisoning (the elderly, pregnant women, young
children and those suffering from immune deficiency
diseases) should consult their doctor with any concerns about
eating raw eggs.

OVEN GUIDE: You may find cooking times vary depending
on the oven you are using. For fan-forced ovens, as a general
rule, set the oven temperature to 20°C (35°F) lower than
indicated in the recipe.